ADVANCE PRA

"*InCitations* will not tell you all of life's answers boiled down to one phrase like some over-praised, over-priced 'self-help' book. It will, however, provoke you to think and question how you see and interact with the people around you.

The author explores everything from behavioural economics, complexity theory, sport, mythology, humour, advertising and TV with a sense of humility that is refreshing and approachable. The more challenging content in each section is followed by a realistic reflection and breakdown of how to apply the topic to your own work or life. This moreish diversity of citing everything from current pop culture to world-renowned physicists keeps the reader wanting to read 'just one more section.'"

Krista Bradley,
Senior Manager Market Research,
Microsoft

"Tas's book is a really accessible read, reminiscent of the type of journey that Bill Bryson takes you on – conversational and easy to absorb, yet still interesting and educational. I normally wouldn't be tempted to pick up a book of quotes but thankfully this is so much more than that."

Charlotte Vlahavas
Senior Retention Manager,
The Daily Telegraph

"In his elegantly and eloquently written third book, Tas once again displays his storytelling virtuosity to give you tools and evidence that you can rip off and claim as your own."

James Max
TalkRADIO Presenter,
columnist for the *Financial Times* and
The Spectator, and business strategy advisor

"A veritable feast of memorable quotes and aphorisms, dissected, contextualized and woven into a nifty little guide to dropping pearls of well-informed insight into conversation to make you seem cleverer than you really are."

Louise Halliday
Director of External Affairs,
Royal Albert Hall

"Another gloriously eclectic selection from the marvellously idiosyncratic cerebral wanderings of Tas. As always, much to inspire, energize and chuckle over. Top stuff!"

Richard Swaab
Deputy Chairman,
AMV BBDO agency

"A wonderful treatise on why and when to ignite your words and thinking, and an eclectic collection of ideas and reflections as told by a bona fide storyteller."

Daniel Moore
Senior Speaker Consultant,
Celebrity Speakers

"There is a Chinese proverb – knowledge is the best charity. Whether you are stuck or eager to express yourselves, this series of memorable quotes, aphorisms and expressions will spark your thinking and communication. *InCitations* is also a meaningful gift to share with the person you cherish."

Katie Zhou
Co Founder and Managing Director,
MetaThink Strategic Branding
& Innovation Consultancy

"Tasgal's luscious love of language is infectious and pulls you in. His considered and comical exposition of branding, phrase origins and the behavioural insights they unearth is a 'must read' for wordsmiths and self-confessed smart-asses alike."

Eimear Duffy
Senior Insight Manager,
Consumer Council for Northern Ireland

"From Oscar Wilde to Alan Partridge, from politics to psychoanalysis and from comedy to treasonable tea-pots, you never quite know what to expect next in this beguiling book. That's one of the joys of this wonderful collection of quotes and expressions, illuminated by Tas's insightful research, perceptive observations and natural wit."

Graham Shaw
International speaker
and speaking coach

"My mother tongue is Dutch, but I will definitely incorporate a lot of examples from the book in my writing and speaking to increase my happiness in using, playing and working with words and language. This book is a great summary of tips and tricks for success in any situation where you communicate with others, whether they are colleagues or friends. Thank you, Tas, for increasing the enlightenment in this part of my life!"

Irene Eising
Technical Support Manager,
DSM Nutritional Products

"We often use phrases without knowing where they were first used, their original intent and current relevance. In this book, Tas brings a new grounding to these phrases and sayings to incite us to new and deeper thought and action. An inspiring and enriching read."

Pieter Twine
General Manager Loyalty,
Woolworths and MySchool

"Tas manages to blend quotes from Father Ted, minor French noblemen, Oscar Wilde, Abram Games, Ernest Hemingway and too many others to mention in a book that entertains, informs and provokes discussion in equal measure: I felt compelled to keep going back for more."

Andy Fernandez
Bookshop and Library Manager,
the Chartered Institute of Marketing

"Tas is the very model of an ideas detective. A forensic friend guiding and guarding the intelligent reader through the world of fake news, dodgy data or phoney philosophy. He is both erudite and Araldite: widely read and knowledgeable, yet really sticks to his task, leaving no stone unturned until he sources the true origins of iconic phrases we thought we knew, but can still love – albeit now with the wisdom of knowing their true genesis."

Andy Green
Director, Grow Social Capital

Published by
LID Publishing Limited
The Record Hall, Studio 304,
16-16a Baldwins Gardens,
London EC1N 7RJ, UK

info@lidpublishing.com
www.lidpublishing.com

A member of:

BPR ⊛
businesspublishersroundtable.com

© Anthony Tasgal, 2020
© LID Publishing Limited, 2020

Printed by Gutenberg Press, Malta
ISBN: 978-1-912555-57-4

Cover and Page design: Caroline Li

ANTHONY TASGAL

INCITATIONS

DISCOVERING A WORLD OF INSPIRATION THROUGH QUOTES, WORDS AND EXPRESSIONS

MADRID | MEXICO CITY | LONDON
NEW YORK | BUENOS AIRES
BOGOTA | SHANGHAI | NEW DELHI

CONTENTS

To Will. Not a rabbit.

INTRODUCTION

InCitations is the third part of a loose trilogy centred on the identification and propagation of insight. Whether you are in business, a student, or in need of something to provide a couple of hours of intelligent succour and surprise, I hope this book ends up in your hands.

In *The Storytelling Book*, I wanted to restore the power of human and emotional storytelling to our communications to make them more persuasive, insightful and effective.

With *The Inspiratorium*, the goal was to delve into the nature of insight, especially for those digging at the coalface of marketing and branding, in order to create the ideal environment for our brains to understand and generate insight.

Here, I want to expand on some of those themes.

The title (as a storytelling maven, I naturally attach great weight to a memorable and distinctive headline or title) should make clear my intentions:

to proffer a series of memorable quotes, aphorisms and expressions (that is, citations) and by delving into their history and meaning/s help you find ways of applying – or just pondering on – them in ways that incite insight, and that add to a sense of justifiable smartness.

Think of this book as a snackable range of inspiring quotes, aphorisms and words to illuminate, to trigger debate, conversation and reflection, and enliven and enrich your writing and thinking.

Within these pages, we will try to cover the whole gamut from the arts to the sciences, taking in advertising, psychology, and behavioural economics; myths, framing, and storytelling to the classics, etymology and punctuation; passing via *New Yorker* cartoons, TV series, distracting pigeons, baby shoes, death metal bands and cobblers.

We will encounter wits, writers, lyricists, firebrands, psychoanalysts, complexity theorists, physicists, oracles, carrots, Spartan mothers and tractor boys, and observe the difference between jumbo jets and mayonnaise, the significance of 45 and the meaning of 42, and discover how to brand invertebrates.

A few rules and pledges before we get going:

SOME RULES

1. I've tried to make it a mantra, a principle and a philosophy not to include any statements which could appear on motivational fridge magnets (henceforth known as MFMs) or the sort of lazy shards of so-called wisdom that vast swathes of Twitter users spend their time disseminating

2. The format: each incitation is chunked into three sections: the first part outlines who said it originally and in what context – the story of the quote. The second explores why they said it and what were the reasons for its selection and its enduring relevance. The third section suggests how it can be used in presentations or in everyday life in ways that will provoke insight and reflection

3. There are tags for each section, so you can explore different themes that emerge throughout the collection

SOME PLEDGES

1. Even with a fair wind and a following sea, this book won't help you overcome adversity or help you find the real you, assuming you're unhappy with the unreal you

2. I should declare upfront that the idea of this book is definitely not 'to begin each day with a quote that will convince you that it's going to be an even better day than the one before'

3. Or that 'inside you is a diamond core of strength that helps you achieve anything you put your mind to'. Neither will there be 'uplifting statements to help you shine as the amazing individual you are'. Neither can I affirm that anything contained herein will provide validation that 'you rock'

4. I can't promise that the contents will make your jaw drop, help you energize yourself, bring you inner peace, touch your heart and empower your soul or make it shine, or that the book will offer affirmations of compassion, provide a celebration of grandfathers everywhere, or will honour great husbands/wives/mothers/basketball coaches

5. It's unlikely to help you relax and unwind, radiate positivity, embolden, uplift or renew your spirit (unless your spirit is a library book), or even assist

you in your bid for domestic/corporate/global leadership inside or outside of the boardroom, bedroom or bathroom

6. It will almost certainly fail to make you calmer or believe in yourself; there is only an outside chance it will offset the meaningless anomie of existence or give emotional succour if you are friendless, let alone break up your typical day (does it really need to be disassembled?) or inspire your best year ever

7. You may have come to a point in your life where you need your life summed up in one metaphor (a bicycle, a box of chocolates, a camera, a cheeseburger, drinking Prosecco) but I have nothing relevant to offer

8. Any winning that happens will in all likelihood be incidental

9. My publishers (with all the might of their legal team) have discouraged me from promising you anything that might be deemed to be 'life-changing' in the way of personal or professional success, in life, business or sport (are they mutually exclusive?)

10. There are no exhortations to be kind, as this seems largely self-evident

11. If you are the sort of person seeking reassurances to have hope and be strong, or to live hard/ your dreams or with intention; to laugh loud/ be humble/smile often, seize the day (ideally in Latin) and never give up, then it is best you move on promptly

12. If you need someone to remind you that you are amazing and/or loved, I am not that person

13. Neither will you find any colouring to be done in these pages, or anything I would knowingly affix the word 'iconic' to

14. If you are affected by crippling doubt, I am not sure I can help you either

15. If you are expecting to see vapid homilies about love or anything equally life-affirming, this may not be the work for you, but do think deeply about whether it might make a suitable gift for someone in the office who likes that sort of thing

16. You may indeed be beautiful, but I have no way of knowing so I am avoiding the topic

17. If you want to dance in the rain, there is probably nothing I can do to deter you so go ahead

18. If you feel your husband is hotter than your coffee, you have my wholehearted endorsement, but there is really little else I can help you with other than suggesting you reheat your coffee

19. Feel free to eat dessert first. But I'd steer clear of having chilli after

20. Consulting this work will definitely not make you better off financially: technically you will be slightly *worse* off in pecuniary terms

21. No lemons have been squeezed during the making of this book

22. And if you are on a journey, all I can offer is hope that you have the correct ticket and appropriate underwear

1. "THERE IS AS MUCH DIFFERENCE BETWEEN US AND OURSELVES AS THERE IS BETWEEN US AND OTHERS"

A) WHO SAID IT AND IN WHAT CONTEXT

Michel de Montaigne (1533-1592) was a minor French nobleman, as well as a lawyer, mayor and advisor to kings during a time of profound religious unrest.

But it is as a philosopher and an essayist that history judges him. He is generally considered to be the inventor of the essay and for this he is lionized as something of a hero of the Enlightenment. For some critics, the first thinker – and perhaps it's not too outré to call him the first blogger.

He devoted himself to introspection, writing about the self – himself – and addressing deep and contemporary issues such as identity, scepticism and selfhood, and was deeply critical of philosophical arrogance. He is often labelled the sceptic's sceptic and was happy to attack the pedantry and arrogance of those he regarded as pseudo-intellectuals. As well as being intellectually provocative, he could be obscenely explicit.

B) WHY THEY SAID IT

This incitation comes from Book II of his 107 *essais* (the French word also contains a spirit of 'attempts' or 'trials').

Montaigne was hostile to the idea of dogmatic certainty, favoured a Socratic humility, and the world of 'infinite confusion'. His very personal observations about identity chime with contemporary neuroscientists and writers about the brain who cite Montaigne for this extraordinarily advanced insight into personality and identity.

But he was also modest and droll, reminding us that we are all 'blockheads' and *"On the highest throne in the world, we are seated, still, upon our arses."*

C) WHEN YOU SHOULD USE IT

Nowadays with all the wisdom that comes from self-help manuals and YouTube gurus, we are often seduced by the idea that the self is a concrete, immutable 'thing' – what philosopher Julian Baggini in *The Ego Trick* calls the "pearl or essence of self" – and to "find our true, unified and substantial self".

This goes back to the inscription on the door of the oracle at Delphi in Greece – 'Gnothi seauton', meaning 'know thyself'. (See Number 16).

But this assumes there is one fixed self that can be known.

- Don't fall into the trap of assuming and adopting a 'fixed mindset'. As psychologist Carol Dweck describes it, always seek to have a 'growth mindset' and see yourself as perpetually changing, adapting and in flux rather than who you have been and who you will remain

- One application that should be posted up on the noticeboards (or digital equivalents) is to bear in mind that 'consumer' – that dated behaviourist label for people who we want to buy our stuff with unfettered loyalty and fervour – is not a one-person-fits-all. So, asking people in market research will only get superficial responses to the 'real self' as so often that will change by context and mood

- In terms of personal development, we have to accept that we are 'many mes' and that we are con-stantly reinventing ourselves. Baggini prefers the metaphor of the self as a cloud, always moving and shifting, albeit with a limited sense of psychologi-cal continuity

- If we are indeed best seen as players on a stage, we need direction and guidance with our roles to (even) find what is the right role for us

TAGS: identity, personality, behaviour change, education, happiness, self-development

2. "THE MONSTROUS WORSHIP OF FACTS"

Probably not one of his most magnet-worthy sayings; Oscar Wilde coined this plangent warning in an 1891 essay called *The Decay of Lying*, a conversational piece modelled on Plato's Socratic dialogues, but featuring, instead of Athens' most notorious nuisance and a selection of interlocutors, Wilde's own sons, Cyril and Vivian.

> *"If something cannot be done to check, or at least to modify, our monstrous worship of facts, Art will become sterile and beauty will pass away from the land."*

Wilde is actually criticizing the obsession with factuality as an impediment to the act of writing, an obstacle to creativity, art and beauty. Common at the time was the notion that to get back to nature is to get back to reality. Wilde was vehemently opposed to this, suggesting in his cheerfully provocative way that dull truths and facts are impediments to the creative spirit. All art was a form of lying for Wilde.

Art should be detached from reality and beauty from purpose, he proposes. It is a special and admirable form of lying, and that art holds up the mirror to life. Art doesn't reflect the times, he goes as far to say, but art creates the style and mood of the moment. Life in fact copies art and art does not reflect the times, it creates them.

B) WHY THEY SAID IT

According to Wilde's playfully provocative essay, lying – the telling of beautiful untrue things – is the true and proper aim of art.

Of the many targets he aims at, one is the reverential insistence on the elevation of fact and truth at the expense of the imaginative impulse. All creativity is falsehood: there is no Mother of Dragons, the boy wizard didn't really exist and – spoiler alert – Alexander Hamilton didn't actually rap.

> *"Facts are not merely finding a footing-place in history, but they are usurping the domain of Fancy, and have invaded the kingdom of Romance. Their chilling touch is over everything. They are vulgarising mankind."*

Wilde is also targeting the English obsession with facts, satirized by Dickens's character Thomas Gradgrind in *Hard Times*, who stated:

"Now, what I want is, Facts. Teach these boys and girls nothing but Facts. Facts alone are wanted in life." (1.1.1)

The fact (sic) that Dickens chooses to open the novel with a statement about the importance of facts is a demonstration of his belief (as with Wilde) that facts are never enough.

C) WHEN YOU SHOULD USE IT

These days, I would argue, his words ring ever more truthful especially if we are trying to make business more successful and our lives more fulfilling, creative and happy.

So:

- Accept (even if for a hypothetical moment) that facts and truth are grey and inert. Creativity is vibrant, colourful and joyous

- When we are trying to imagine something new, conjure up novelty and genuinely attempt to break barriers and seek blue skies; can we acknowledge that facts will only get us so far and actually, willingly, and knowingly let go of them?

- If you seek beauty, never assume that it is the same as truth. Only bad art is based on reality

- Can we start accepting that the monstrous worship of targets, metrics, KPIs and ROIs is crippling our ability to be different, to be happy and to be spontaneous?

- The entire education system in many countries has fallen prey to this monstrous worship, so children become crammed to bursting with facts so that they pass the tests the system subjects them to rather than becoming playful, inquisitive and provocative thinkers. When schools are transformed into exam factories, individuality and creativity can never flourish

- And let's be Wilde-r in our thinking: famed for his love of paradox and incongruity, let's also allow ourselves to dwell more on 'what ifs'

TAGS: play, provocation, art vs science, persuasion, happiness, education

3. "IF YOU DISGUISE EXPOSITION WITH 'EMOTIONAL OVERLAY', IT'S RENDERED UNDETECTABLE"

A) WHO SAID IT AND IN WHAT CONTEXT

Jed Mercurio is one of the UK's leading TV writers, as well as being a producer, director and novelist. He is perhaps best known for being the creator and showrunner of the BBC police procedural-cum-crime-thriller series, *Line of Duty*. Starting in 2012, it focuses on an internal anticorruption unit called AC-12. Over five series (with a sixth already commissioned), it has won pretty much every TV award and deservedly remains one of the BBC's 'jewels in the crown'. Arguably, 2018's most water cooler, gossip-worthy TV event in the UK was Mercurio's BBC series *The Bodyguard*, which had the nation (and beyond) hanging onto every cliff and achieved the highest viewing figures for a new BBC drama in the multichannel era and the highest BBC viewing figures since 2008. It received the highest accolade in 2018, being used in the BBC's *Comic Relief* as a centrepiece sketch featuring the characters.

So Mercurio knows a thing or two about writing, drama, suspense and involvement.

The incitation is mentioned in John Yorke's 2013 dissection of storytelling, *Into The Woods*. (As well as being an author, Yorke himself is a TV hyphenate – a writer and producer, returning as executive producer of the long-running BBC soap *EastEnders* in 2017.)

B) WHY THEY SAID IT

Yorke cites the comment from Mercurio based on an email exchange in the midst of a discussion on the nature of exposition and character, and the need to create reason and desire.

He argues that exposition – telling – has to be handled carefully. Raw exposition – telling people 'stuff' (yes, I'm talking about you, content providers) – can achieve precisely the opposite to the goal it seeks by failing to engage the emotions, and therefore risks being filtered out.

Good dialogue, in Yorke's elegant expression, is forged in the furnace of opposition.

C) WHEN YOU SHOULD USE IT

Yorke and Mercurio are clearly concentrating primarily on dramatic writing, but the arguments work for all forms of communication. Exposition also needs conflict (the fuel of drama). So, for anyone working in communications, this quote should remind us of several important and noteworthy lessons.

- We may be conditioned in some quarters (business, education, politics) to be wary or disdainful of emotion, thinking that it has no place in domains which rely on the sacred purity of informational evaluation

- But this flies in the face of advice from writers, storytellers like Mercurio and Yorke, as well as scientists of all hues who consistently and cogently argue that our humanity depends on 'emotional overlay'. As Mercurio highlights, exposition is essential in all forms of communication, but if it becomes overt, explicit and ostentatious we resist it

- Instead – as Oscar Wilde reminded us earlier (Number 2) – make sure that the rational fact-bearing load is disguised and lathered with emotion, dialogue and desire

- Never rely on exposition, the dry transmission of facts and information. Telling is not selling, show not tell – these are clichés for good reason

- So, let's remember that substance needs style, content depends on form

- This will create conflict and set the pulse racing of your audience: the brain – especially the emotional, spontaneous, instinctive beating heart of System 1 – relishes a good scrap, an argument, a struggle

TAGS: storytelling, persuasion, behaviour change

4. "WHEN YOU MEET SOMEBODY FOR THE FIRST TIME, YOU'RE NOT MEETING THEM …"

"Relationships, easy to get into, hard to maintain. Why are they so hard to maintain? Because it's hard to keep up the lie! Cause you can't get nobody being you. You got to lie to get somebody. You can't get nobody looking like you look, acting like you act, sounding like you sound. When you meet somebody for the first time, you're not meeting them. You're meeting their representative."

A) WHO SAID IT AND IN WHAT CONTEXT

American comic, Chris Rock – more accurately, another writer, director and producer – was one of the great *Saturday Night Live* (SNL) alumni of the 1990s before treading the common path of many SNL stars: going into movies, creating sitcoms (*Everybody Hates Chris* 2005-2009) and moving into animated movie voiceovers (for example, as Marty the Zebra in the DreamWorks *Madagascar* series), as well as hosting the Oscars in 2005 and 2016.

The quote comes from one of his HBO specials recorded at the Apollo Theatre, Harlem on 10 July 1999, *Bigger and Blacker*.

B) WHY THEY SAID IT

Rock's routine here is about love, marriage, first impressions and relationships, but most significantly and memorably deals with the lies, deception and self-deception that is part of human relationships and self-awareness.

He is succinctly highlighting how the first flush of meeting, the desire to portray oneself in the most desirable (yes, flattering) light, leads to a certain down-weighting of reality.

He is not the first comedian or counsellor to note that it will also give way to the boredom and tedium (to use one of the psychological terms – adaptation) of long-term relationships.

The filmmaker and comedy legend (not an unfair ascription), Mel Brooks, said something similar:

> *"You're always a little disappointing in person because you can't be the edited essence of yourself."*

C) WHEN YOU SHOULD USE IT

As with the de Montaigne incitation (Number 1), we are in the area of self-knowledge, truth and deception.

So:

- Those embarking on the dating game would do well to realize that they are indeed not meeting the person of their dreams, but the representative, advertising executive or PR manager of that person. Equally, they will be playing the same game themselves. PR meets PR and let's accept that reality

- This is why social media has become so integral to communication. In the language of evolutionary psychology, the likes of Facebook, Instagram and Twitter can often be seen as advertisements for our desires and dreams and social and sexual signals to potential mates

- Too often we fear authenticity and honesty, but perhaps acknowledging when we are being our own representative might reduce the chances of mismatch

- Which is why, again, we need to understand the importance of everything that is not rational, explicit and factual. As the behavioural economics enterprise seeks to remind us, we are not simply a library of facts, declarations and needs: we are a subtle and fragile compendium of what lies beneath, what we are barely aware of and an honest assessment of that status would be to everyone's benefit

TAGS: identity, personality, behaviour change, education, happiness, self-development

"TFBUNDY"

WHO SAID IT AND IN WHAT CONTEXT

Dr Adam Fox is a children's allergist and consultant at Guy's and St Thomas' hospital in London. He has been on something of a crusade to bring to the public some examples of doctors' slang and why it is used.

Some are acronyms, many are euphemisms, but all show extraordinary ingenuity, given the pressures that doctors are under (and the common misconception about those of a scientific bent lacking the raw materials for a sense of humour). A short selection should demonstrate their inventiveness:

- Bobbing for apples: unblocking a badly consti-pated patient with one's finger

- Bury the hatchet: to accidentally leave a surgical instrument inside a patient

- Code brown: Incontinence-related emergency

- CRAFT: Can't Remember a F*cking Thing

- DBI: Dirtbag index, which is calculated by the number of tattoos on the body multiplied by the number of recent missing teeth, to estimate the number of days without a bath

- Freud Squad: code for psychiatrists

- GPO: Good for Parts Only

- The Journal of Anecdotal Medicine: The source to quote for less than wholly evidence-based medical facts

- Neuro-faecal Syndrome: S**t for brains

- Organ recital: A hypochondriac's medical history

- Pumpkin positive: Refers to the implication that if a penlight were shone into the patient's mouth, it would reveal a brain so small that the whole head would light up

- TEETH: Tried Everything Else, Try Homeopathy

- TFBUNDY: Totally F*cked But Unfortunately Not Dead Yet

- UBI: Unexplained beer injury, for all those hungover people on Sunday mornings with black eyes or swollen knees and no idea how they've got them

- Whopper with cheese: an obese woman with yeast infection

- Digging for worms: carrying out varicose vein surgery

- Departure lounge: the geriatric ward

B) WHY THEY SAID IT

Lamenting the obsolescence of these colourful descriptions, Dr Fox explained:

> "Humour is a way of coping with patients' distress at loss, grief, disease and death. I predicted years ago that medical slang was dying out and that does seem to be happening. Partly it's because patients can now access their medical records, so such slang terms are no longer written down."

They all show the classic signs of jargon: language which is used as the preserve of an elite few in order to reinforce tribal norms against outsiders (in this case patients, or the elements of the medical or pseudo-medical fraternity such as psychiatrists, practitioners of homeopathy, or even anaesthetists and general surgeons referred to as 'Gassers' and 'Slashers' respectively).

So, although they may appear from the outside to be arcane medical terminology, they turn out to be something entirely different. Some, it is fair to say, should probably not be used in medical notes.

Dr Fox recounts the tale of one doctor who had scribbled TTFO – for 'Told To F*ck Off' – on a patient's notes. When asked by a judge what the acronym meant, he had the presence of mind to extemporize: 'To take fluids orally'.

Some even reflect geographical prejudices: the most famous being NFN – Normal for Norfolk (see Number 6, below).

And in case we think that science and medicine are incompatible with humour, a glance at *The Sunday Times* bestseller list in 2018 in the UK showed that it was largely dominated by *This Is Going to Hurt* by Adam Kay.

After its publication in September 2017, Kay's book was translated into 20 languages and won numerous awards including *The Sunday Times* 'Humour Book of the Year'. It was universally acclaimed as "painfully funny" by Stephen Fry and "heartbreaking and hilarious" by Charlie Brooker and was set to be turned into a TV series on BBC2, as well as a national theatre tour. A deeply personal account of the life of a junior doctor in the UK's National Health Service, it was laugh-out-loud funny, as well as a perceptive analysis of the highs and lows of the system. The sequel, *Twas the Nightshift Before Christmas*, was equally successful in 2019.

c) WHEN YOU SHOULD USE IT

- Jargon is usually a baneful, joyless experience, especially in the corporate world. Even in other disciplines, the desire to import some of the 'thinking' and systematic rationalism of management consultants has led to an exponential growth in nonsensical jargon, usually as a cover for having nothing new or enlightening to say, but a desire to be paid for it

- Yet as Doctors' Slang proves, jargon can also be a source of wit and imagination steeped with satirical intent

- If we feel the need to use jargon, either to show off our tribal smarts, creating a community of language, or even show the hoi polloi why we charge so much, why can't we at least try to emulate Doctors' Slang?

TAGS: language, humour, jargon

6. "NORMAL FOR NORFOLK"

A) WHO SAID IT AND IN WHAT CONTEXT

As we have just seen with Doctors' Slang, there are a number of expressions the medical profession has coined to give an ironic, jaundiced or pejorative (depending on your view) slant on patients.

One geographical acronym that occurs with great frequency is NFN, standing for Normal For Norfolk. This shorthand is intended to designate (or imply) a certain medical – or more often a mental short-coming – associated with this rustic part of England, with insinuations of inbreeding often associated with other parts of the world (e.g. 'rednecks' in the US).

According to Keith Skipper, a local broadcaster, entertainer and the founder of Friends of Norfolk Dialect, these doctors were in all probability 'fur-riners' (sic) or people from outside the county, an expression which also highlights the very much non-RP (Received Pronunciation or 'speaking posh') accent of that part of the UK, a kingdom that is anything but united in terms of dialects and accents.

B) WHY THEY SAID IT

Norfolk is famous for being quite isolated – it has no motorways and the journey time from London to parts of Norfolk could also get you to Paris – which seems to breed a sort of insular pride and cussedness.

An example of the NFN attitude includes a police recording of a car being driven in Great Yarmouth with a wardrobe strapped to its top with nothing more than bubble wrap, and farmers in Aylsham hiring students to dress up as scarecrows. The farmers in question claimed this was a more successful stratagem than might have been expected.

The expression itself became the title of a BBC documentary from 2016-2017, a recent addition to the sub-genre of reality TV programmes dealing with what might be termed 'posh rural aristocrats willing to trade dignity for money'.

Other notable examples of squirearchy-baiting include *The F***ing Fulfords*, a Channel 4 reality programme from 2004 featuring Francis Fulford, the Lord of the Manor of Great Fulford, who inherited 3,000 acres of prime Devon real estate, returning later in the aptly named series *Life is Toff*. ('Toff' itself is a derogatory expression for someone who is posh, perhaps coming from the word 'tuft', a special tassel worn by graduates of Oxbridge colleges whose fathers were peers with votes in the House of Lords.)

The BBC commissioned the first series of *Normal for Norfolk* in 2015, following life at Wiveton Hall under the eccentric tutelage and caterpillar eyebrows of Desmond MacCarthy, living with his 99-year-old mother Chloe.

In what might otherwise have been called 'Pimp My Hall', the gentleman farmer finds ingenious solutions to keeping his 17th century pile intact and his farm a going concern.

c) WHEN YOU SHOULD USE IT

Yet for all this class-based, geo-social condescension, recent data from Public Health England suggests that residents of this maligned county will enjoy six months extra lifespan compared to other parts of England and will be noticeably happier. And Norfolk has more than its share of genius, especially in the field of comedy.

Charlie Higson, one of the creators of *The Fast Show* (1994-2014), actor, novelist and creator of the *Young Bond* franchise attended the University of East Anglia in Norwich; at one point he squatted in London and decorated the house of another scion of East Anglia and polymath, Stephen Fry, who himself grew up in the village of Booton near Reepham, in Norfolk.

The musician James Blunt spent time living in Cley by the Sea and (according to Norfolk Tourism) Aussie-Hollywood royalty Hugh Jackman and Naomi Watts both have mums living in the county.

Actor Rupert Everett was born in the county but, sadly, Grant 'The Flash' Gustin wasn't (the website

Ranker.com failing to distinguish between Norfolk, England and Norfolk, Virginia).

So:

- Let's be careful not to apply the tarred brush too evenly across populations: even much maligned Norfolk has its fair share of geniuses, eccentric or not

- Let's cherish and nurture those quirks, foibles and eccentricities and not unnecessarily demonize the socially maladroit or painfully posh but instead celebrate unconventionality

TAGS: demographics, humour, conventionality, acronyms

7. "THE TRACTOR BOYS"

A) WHO SAID IT AND IN WHAT CONTEXT

If we move southwards from Norfolk to Suffolk, we can isolate another example of linguistic guile and aptitude.

Suffolk was once home to a famous top-tier football team, Ipswich Town, who currently play in the second level Championship alongside local rivals, Norwich City.

In their glory years, in the top flight of English football/soccer in the Premier League in 2000-2001 and 2001-2002, Ipswich Town were self-deprecatingly honest about their lack of fashionability and scale compared to the likes of football aristocracy such as Manchester United, Liverpool or Chelsea. Around this time, they started referring to themselves in an agricultural vein as 'The Tractor Boys'.

B) WHY THEY SAID IT

As with many origin stories there are a number of variants of how it began. One suggests the fans of Leeds sang it in amazement that they were being beaten by a 'bunch of tractor drivers'.

But according to local newspaper, the *Ipswich Star*, when reporting on his death in September 2011, the chant was devised by one Claude Chapman. He is said to have been watching his local team compete in the Carlsberg Pub Cup in 2000 at Liverpool FC's famous Anfield stadium when, after a goal was scored, he yelled out "two-nil to the tractor boys".

(For non-football/soccer fans, this was itself a riff on Arsenal fans who used to chant 'One nil to the Arsenal' to the chorus of the Pet Shop Boys 1992 version of the Village People's 1979 hit Go West).

This chant proved popular with Ipswich Town fans who made it their anthem at Portman Road. Not all Ipswich managers and fans appreciated the 'country bumpkin' image but it has stuck.

The local derby between Ipswich and Norwich is known jokingly as the Old Farm Derby: note for non (UK) football fans – this is a play on the great Glasgow Scottish football/soccer rivalry between the two Glasgow clubs Rangers and Celtic, traditionally referred to as the Auld Firm Derby – known as the oldest local rivalry in UK football, and the 'second-fiercest' (how is that measured?) after the Midlands derby between West Bromwich Albion and Wolverhampton Wanderers.

The Ipswich-Norwich fierceness may be down to the fact that each team represents their entire county:

unlike say in London, where there are always several teams represented in the top division. The winners can claim to be entitled to unofficially call themselves the 'Pride of Anglia'.

It has also generated one of my favourite gems of wordplay. What do you call a former Ipswich supporter? An ex tractor fan.

c) WHEN YOU SHOULD USE IT

- This should remind us that rivalry is a sign of and a result of local geography, and that within bounds it is all perfectly healthy

- And local rivalry will always be the source of ingenuity and humour

TAGS: demographics, humour, conventionality

8. "KNOWING ME, KNOWING YOU, AHA!"

A) WHO SAID IT AND IN WHAT CONTEXT

And perhaps Norfolk's most famous comic creation is Alan Partridge. From his debut as a maladroit, hapless and self-unaware sports reporter on BBC Radio 4's programme *On the Hour* to the BBC TV series *I'm Alan Partridge* and his big screen debut in *Alpha Papa* (2013) and a series of books, including his autobiography *I Partridge* and *Nomad* to the 2019 series *This Time with Alan Partridge* he has become a familiar character for his foibles and parodic amusement.

Armando Iannucci, one of the writers involved in the creation of the Partridge character alongside Steve Coogan, Chris Morris, Rebecca Front, Peter Baynham and Patrick Marber said that Norwich was chosen as his home because it was, *"Geographically just that little bit annoyingly too far from London and has this weird kind of isolated feel that seemed right for Alan."*

Many other Partridge clips are fan favourites, including the famous 'Dan' scene where Partridge is in a car park and recognizes and calls out repeatedly to a kitchen salesman, Dan Moody. They had met earlier and discovered they both liked the same beer, used the same deodorant and drove Lexi ('the plural of Lexus').

B) WHY THEY SAID IT

More a comedy of character than catchphrases, Partridge is nevertheless associated with the cry 'Aha!'. This goes back to the spoof BBC chat show – 'Knowing Me, Knowing You', after the Abba song, with its 'Aha!' climax.

The Abba song was written in 1976 and is one of a number they recorded on the theme of relationship breakups (or breakdowns). It was the biggest single in the UK in 1977 and was directed – as were many other Abba videos – by Lasse Hallström, who later went to Hollywood and whose filmography covers *My Life as a Dog*, *What's Eating Gilbert Grape*, *The Cider House Rules* and *Chocolat*.

Before Abba, we can look at the 'Aha moment', otherwise known as the 'Eureka moment', the explosive sense of recognition or flash of understanding. In *The Inspiratorium* I explored the nature and varieties of insight and its origin with the story of Archimedes and 'eureka' (Greek for 'I have found it', once he realized he had solved the problem set for him by King Hiero of Syracuse).

The *Oxford English Dictionary* traces an early German use of the phrase ('Aha-Erlebnis') to 1908 and notes its use in English in the 1930s.

In one recent legal development, in the US Oprah Winfrey had been engaged in a dispute with the insurance and financial services company Mutual of Omaha. On her TV programme and across other media channels, Oprah talks of 'aha moments' and invites guests to share theirs. In 2009, the insurance giant started using 'Official sponsor of the aha moment' in their advertising. Winfrey objected that viewers would imagine some connection with her programme, so the matter came to court where it was (mutually?) resolved.

This is another instance of when brands try to own and copyright bits of language that we would like to think reside in the common domain.

C) WHEN YOU SHOULD USE IT

- We all need and search for 'aha' moments in our lives

- We laugh at Alan Partridge, but as with so much humour beneath lies the insight and wit of truth told. Many of us are not blessed with great self-awareness; many of us are trying to make up for social deficiencies, and like so many other comic creations, from *Dad's Army*'s Captain Mainwaring to Basil Fawlty to *The Office*'s David Brent, there is an educational element: beware arrogance, assume humility and learn from your mistakes

TAGS: insight, humour, language

9. "THE MOST JEWISH JOKE"

A) WHO SAID IT AND IN WHAT CONTEXT

In August 2017, comedian Jerry Seinfeld appeared on the Norm Macdonald show/podcast, Macdonald being another comic and former *Saturday Night Live* cast member alongside Chris Rock.

On the show Seinfeld announces, "This is the greatest Jew joke I've ever heard, and I love that," – he goes on to warn Macdonald – "You're not going to get it, but that's the joke."

"Two gentile businessmen meet on the street, one says, 'How's business?' The other says, 'Great!'"

If you don't find yourself LOL-ing uncontrollably at this point let me explain.

Any Jewish person worth their lox would instinctively know that two Jewish businessmen (actually any two random Jews, certainly over a certain age) would never greet each other in this way. The accepted proper response to 'How's business' would (of course) be a resigned shrug, a vexed 'oy vey' or some other exhibition of kvetching (complaining). It is not in the Jewish DNA to declare optimistically that 'things are great', something that feels more natural in the mouth of a forward-thinking, go-getting, hope-filled WASP.

B) WHY THEY SAID IT

Part of what makes it funny, as Seinfeld points out, is about who gets it. The irony here being that this is a candidate for the 'greatest Jewish joke ever' without actually featuring any Jewish people in it.

So, as with so much humour, this is a joke that is about the nature and role of comedy itself: what makes some of us (at least) laugh and what it says about tribal belonging and attachment.

Seinfeld is using the joke as a live demonstration of the polarizing effect of jokes in terms of in-group and out-group affiliation. The joke here operates as a cultural totem, a tribal watchword, a password or touchstone for tribal identification.

C) WHEN YOU SHOULD USE IT

- Humour can be the most elegant and incisive way of unearthing insight

- It also certainly functions as a code or signal for 'are you one of us?' Jokes are literally about 'did you get it?', meaning 'did you understand?', or are you smart enough or otherwise qualified to be 'one of us'

- In marketing, what are brands if not shibboleths (see Number 55 below)? As a way of signalling our status and exploring ways to evolutionary success, brands have become a way of defining ourselves as part of what I term 'tribes of shared meaning'

- Seinfeld's joke should also remind us that often in communication what is missing is as vital as what is present or explicit. Too often we are so concerned about what we say, we underestimate the importance of what is left unsaid

TAGS: insight, humour, art, language, signalling

10. "HOW'S YOUR WIFE?" "COMPARED TO WHAT?"

A) WHO SAID IT AND IN WHAT CONTEXT

I found this joke in the most unlikely source, in philosopher and cognitive scientist Daniel Dennett's *Darwin's Dangerous Idea*, his exploration of the modern Darwinian synthesis.

After carrying out excavations, I can reveal it was in fact created by Henny Youngman, a celebrated English-American comedian (1906-1998), known as 'The King of One-Liners'. Much of his output is still current, some gags having even made it into *Bartlett's Familiar Quotations*, the definitive US compendium of quotations and sayings.

But I think the joke operates on another level, which makes it more versatile.

It is about the process known as 'framing'. The joke also works because it asks us to question our linguistic and perceptual assumptions: 'How's your wife' does indeed have more than one possible response depending on the frame or context you are applying.

B) WHY THEY SAID IT

At the time, Youngman's motives were simple: to make his audience laugh. Youngman was gigging and gagging during the golden age of US comics, from Milton Berle to Mel Brooks, Woody Allen, Neil Simon and other writers and performers working and writing for radio and the newfangled medium that was TV (for example, on *The Sid Caesar Show*).

Many of his gags were at the expense of his wife, who seemed happy for him to make her the butt of many of his bons mots.

"I miss my wife's cooking – as often as I can."; "I take my wife everywhere, but she always finds her way home."

One of Youngman's one-liners that did make it into Bartlett's' was: "Take my wife. Please." – (one that might seem to have aged less well than most of his oeuvre).

C) WHEN YOU SHOULD USE IT

- At the superficial level, the joke works because – as with most humour – it asks us to confront something which we take for granted and leave unexamined. Without thinking we take the question to be an idle enquiry as to the health or welfare of our spouse. The joke plays on this discrepancy

- There are many examples of framing used in two of my favourite domains: behavioural economics, the discipline concerned with how decisions can be optimized; and in storytelling

- Framing is also a core piece in the behavioural economics jigsaw for demonstrating how the framing of information can make an enormous difference: that content (especially hard, rational facts processed cognitively) can be framed or presented in different ways which will create different emotional responses. Another way in which we constantly undervalue form over content

- Brands and their advertising agencies are eminent deployers of this tactic. The retailer Marks and Spencer reframed a £10 meal deal, so that it was positioned not against other rival supermarket meal deal offers, but against the idea – and cost – of eating out in (more expensively-perceived) restaurants

- Perhaps the most refreshing use of reframing is a canny piece of perceptual readjustment for Trojan condoms in the US. Rather than positioning itself against other contraceptive brands or talking generically about the end benefits (as it were), it goes for creating surprise by reframing against the cost of having a baby: Trojan condoms $3.25 versus Huggies diapers/nappies for $22. This creates a double whammy in pushing both emotional and rational buttons in the brain

- So, whether it is a price offer, a suggestion or a research methodology, it always pays to ask, "Compared to what?"

TAGS: language, behaviour change, advertising

11. "WHY HAVE COTTON WHEN YOU CAN HAVE SILK?"

A) WHO SAID IT AND IN WHAT CONTEXT

This was an advertising strapline (or slogan) for the Galaxy brand, the Mars chocolate bar first manufactured in the UK in 1960, but also sold and known in many other countries as Dove.

The line was created in 1987 alongside an ad set to the languorous 'Rhapsody in Blue' composed in 1924 by George Gershwin, which had been given a new lease of life after opening up and featuring throughout Woody Allen's 1979 masterpiece, *Manhattan*. The brief for the ad would have been something like 'unabashed elegance and indulgence as a woman with heels and gloves sensuously unwraps and enjoys her Galaxy with stereotyped furtiveness and intensity'.

As is the case in the notoriously cyclical ad world, the line was revived by agency AMV BBDO in 2013 to support a relaunch emphasizing values of sensuality and smoothness, as epitomized by a CGI Audrey Hepburn.

"... sitting on a crowded bus, wondering when she'll be able to indulge in her GALAXY® chocolate bar."

Rather than Gershwin, this time the music is 'Moon River', by Henry Mancini with lyrics written by Johnny Mercer, originally performed by Hepburn in 1961's *Breakfast at Tiffany's*. (Struggles not to use the word 'iconic'.)

B) WHY THEY SAID IT

There are few advertising lines that survive the test of time, that are elegant and concise and even feel touched with a poetic instinct, but this is one of those. As with all great ideas, it compresses a large amount of fact and feeling and wraps it (pun intended) in an elegant metaphorical overlay, as Jed Mercurio might describe it.

Chocolate aficionados (especially in the UK) will generally tell you that Cadbury – though the more popular and mainstream brand – is a fairly straightforward taste. But Galaxy has a creamier, smoother taste and texture. (Though French and Swiss chocolate fiends will not even deign it worthy of the description 'chocolate'.)

So rather than overtly criticize the opposition, a tactic that Brits in particular often find a tad infra dig and unbecoming in the advertising world, the line simply makes a comparison. Most of us know that cotton has many advantages – comfort and ease, for example – but silk is regarded as more exquisite, luxurious and glossy, as well as requiring more care.

Finally, many slogans are affirmative, declarative or hectoring (Do this! Buy this! We're the best!), but the tone of this is more inquisitive and suggestive, which again feels right for the UK sensitivity and our appreciation of the underdog. Yet it still creates a sense that maybe, just maybe, you could be doing better.

And as all storytellers will tell you, the advantages of a question are manifold. Where a statement of fact can leave the brain with nothing to work with (and even encourage counter arguments), a question invites the brain to ponder, to find an answer, to fill in a gap: that's why crosswords and sudokus are eternally popular.

c) WHEN YOU SHOULD USE IT

The moral of this thought is twofold:

- In advertising and branding terms (and that can include your own brand), always try to avoid the didactic rational approach to communicating. Anything that is framed as a question, that invites reflexion, and perhaps even triggers surprise, is going to be more likely to succeed

- The power of the analogy and metaphor; in order to avoid falling into the trap of merely transmitting information and inviting the response of unconscious apathy, consider how to create an analogy or metaphor that resonates. It's no surprise that, several decades ago, UK campaigns like the Smash Martians and the Andrex puppy created such a long-lasting emotional association (as well as lingering in the memory)

- Oh, and if you are really lucky, your strapline will live on in other guises. "Why have cotton …" became the title of a 2018 exhibition on textiles at Arlington Court, a National Trust property in Devon

TAGS: advertising, language, metaphor/analogy

12. "THAT WILL BE $3." "REALLY, WHEN?"

A) WHO SAID IT AND IN WHAT CONTEXT

This was written by Daniel Gilbert, Professor of Psychology at Harvard and author of one of my favourite works, *Stumbling on Happiness*, an international bestseller, full of insights and some good gags (see Number 23). His thesis – at the risk of oversimplifying – is that human beings are poor 'affective forecasters': that is, we are terrible at predicting our future emotional states.

At the end of his book, there is a Q&A with Gilbert, where he is asked what makes him unhappy.

> *"I get snippy and sarcastic when people use language incorrectly. I shouldn't but I do. When a clerk at a store says, 'That will be three dollars,' I say, 'Really, when?' I know, I know I should be shot."*

B) WHY THEY SAID IT

Gilbert's tongue might be buried quite deeply in his cheek here. Apart from anything else, the store assistant can hardly be accused of using language incorrectly (for a start, he literally refrained from saying 'literally'). And if he did, the rest of us are equally culpable, Professor Gilbert.

But what Gilbert has shown here and is worthy of attention – as we point out ceaselessly in this work – is the need to investigate our assumptions. This particular linguistic convention – using a future tense where the present seems more natural – is something that Gilbert is shining a light on as all good comedy does into areas that we take for granted.

C) WHEN YOU SHOULD USE IT

- This witticism serves many functions: as a smart one-liner, a signalling cue, and also as a reminder to always look beneath the surface to gain fresh insight and inspiration

- We have, too, another instance of a popular science writer and academic who realizes the need to amuse and entertain his audience rather than blinding them with science or burying his audience in a lethal blizzard of facts

TAGS: humour, language, behavioural economics

13. "I'M LEAVING YOU."
"WHO IS HE?"

A) WHO SAID IT AND IN WHAT CONTEXT

Steven Pinker is one of today's great scientific popularizers. Some of his more recent and mainstream works include *Enlightenment Now* and *The Better Angels of our Nature*. Prior to that he stuck more closely to his scientific domains of evolutionary psychology, cognitive science and psycholinguistics. He is also a proud Canadian and atheist in the company of non-Canadians Daniel Dennett and Richard Dawkins.

In his first book for a lay audience, *The Language Instinct*, he follows Noam Chomsky (still one of the ten most cited authors in the humanities) in arguing that language is innate, that grammar is universal and stored in a module in the mind, and this is the basis of the universal 'language instinct'. According to Pinker's analysis, thought shapes language not vice versa through something he calls 'mentalese'. But he goes against his hero by emphasizing the Darwinian basis of language acquisition, something that Chomsky resisted.

It is fair to say that Pinker's ideas are not universally accepted (just look up 'language instinct myth') but any journey with Pinker is entertaining and exhilarating, if only for the anecdotes, stories, and jokes which come frequently enough to punctuate any onset of worthiness, but not so often that they feel self-conscious.

B) WHY THEY SAID IT

In *The Language Instinct* he explores how the brain can create and understand immense complexity in a way that artificial intelligence (AI) still struggles with (in the intervening quarter of a century things have improved with AI, but not to destroy his point).

To demonstrate how our brain is able to compute, create and deconstruct meaning, he gives the following exchange:

WIFE: I'm leaving you.
HUSBAND: Who is he?

Pinker is dramatizing through a simple and amusing aperçu that what makes communication and language so easy for us – and so much harder to programme in AI – is the amount of shared knowledge of the human condition, common sense, as well as mutually-shared details among those engaging in any conversation.

For us it is relatively simple and automatic to intuit that the wife is announcing her intention to abandon her marriage and that the husband goes straight to the nub for him: who is the other man?

These levels of comprehension seem natural to us, but are part of our inherent and universal database and framework of language and meaning.

Pinker, who knows a thing or two about language, has even described language as being a mix of metaphor and combinatorics (the power of permutations to create almost infinite novelty). It is a bridge from the unfamiliar to the familiar.

c) WHEN YOU SHOULD USE IT

- This plays into one of the key strands we are exploring throughout this book: how succinctness and emotion are the key to successful understanding, communication and insight

- So Pinker leads with an amusing and enlightening anecdote, rather than burying it away beneath layers of technical information on grammatology, phonemes and other appurtenances of professors of psycholinguistics and cognitive science

- The moral is that a seemingly slight story, quip, anecdote or metaphor can shed light on something deeper and more complex, and it is preferable to use this approach to invite the lay reader (actually *any* reader) to become involved in what you are trying to convey

- In emotional terms, this is about using the emotions to cut through 'attention spam', in particular via the emotion familiarly known as surprise

- Education systems across the world could learn from this approach

TAGS: humour, language, communication, simplicity, emotion

14. "I'M BLIND, PLEASE HELP."

A) WHO SAID IT AND IN WHAT CONTEXT

Well, who did say it? That is the first question.

The advertising industry likes nothing more than a good story, especially if it's one that enshrines myths about its wisdom and lionizes one of its heroes. Pretty much every copywriter worth their yellow pencil (a famous global advertising award), and a fair few account planners and students of advertising theory will have heard the story of the 'blind man and the sign'.

Most sources still associate it with copywriter, tycoon and industry legend, David Ogilvy – one source headlines it with, 'Why the world's greatest adman added four words to a beggar's sign'.

Born in Surrey, England in 1911, Ogilvy studied history at Oxford before selling cookers as a door-to-door salesman. Here he wrote an instruction manual which was so successful that the young man was offered a position at the Mather and Crowther advertising agency.

From there he was seconded to the US to work at the Gallup research organization where he first developed his deep understanding of human behaviour and how it could be explored: it also helped him in his role in British Intelligence during the Second World War.

After the war, he resumed his vertiginous ascent of the advertising industry, founding his own agency, Ogilvy, Benson and Mather in 1948, with support from his previous employers. From there, with his trademark red braces/suspenders he was renowned as 'The Father of Advertising', though some might accord that honorific to Bill Bernbach, one of the Kings of Madison Avenue, the Mad Men of legend, and one of the most influential thinkers in the history of the business until and beyond his retirement in 1973.

B) WHY THEY SAID IT

So, the story has it that Ogilvy was walking to work one day when he saw a blind beggar. The beggar's sign said 'I'm blind. Please help'. In the retelling, Ogilvy takes the sign and adds something to it. On his return the beggar tells him (or he notices: sources vary) that his cup is now overflowing, so he asks Ogilvy what he added. Ogilvy responds by saying (or showing) that the sign now read:

"It's spring and I'm blind. Please help."

Since then this tale has been told and retold to show the importance of empathy, emotion, storytelling, and the simple ways in which some nifty copywriting can change the world in a slightly uplifting and perhaps patronizing way.

So far, so heart-warming. Except that the story may well be apocryphal and certainly appears to pre-date Ogilvy.

It seems to have been inspired by a poem 'On My Mother's Blindness' by American David Kirby, which itself was based on an incident in the life of a French poet and screenwriter, Jacques Prévert (1900-1977). In this telling, Prévert had written 'Spring is coming but I won't see it'.

(These days that might be mistaken for someone who wasn't fully up to speed with Game of Thrones.)

c) WHEN YOU SHOULD USE IT

- Among other morals, this shows that the power of a huge insight is timelessly memorable. Whether it was a French poet or an Anglo-Scottish-American advertising guru, there is a nugget of truth which still rings true: that instead of adding information, he told a story. And the two words were of a different character altogether

- These days even as people asking for help find themselves in an ultra-competitive market, we witness even more original (?!) examples of this story-fable such as 'why lie, I need a beer' or 'need fuel for Lear jet'

- In a slightly different way, the novelist and essayist E. M. Forster demonstrated in *Aspects of the Novel* the power of two little extra words: "'The king died and then the queen died' is a story. 'The king died, and then the queen died of grief' is a plot." Forster's distinction is that the first version is a series of events in time, whereas the second is overshadowed by a sense of causality

- Always dig. Behind many stories or myths, there is a backstory which is often unexpected

15. "CHANGE YOUR WORDS. CHANGE YOUR WORLD."

WHO SAID IT AND IN WHAT CONTEXT

The timelessness of the David Ogilvy "I'm blind ..." story (or myth or folklore) is evidenced by various recreations. In 2010 a Scottish copywriting and online marketing agency, Purple Feather, released a version of the story, 'The Power of Words'.

It sat unassumingly in a dark and unobtrusive corner of the internet watching the memes go by, until the agency 'seeded it' – as these people are wont to do – at which point, it went on to receive around 25 million views at the time of writing. That's a lot of people who had never even heard of David Ogilvy.

As many have pointed out, in their updated version (and presumably to avoid too much of a legal squabble) the now-female hero writes 'It's a beautiful day and I can't see it'. Which to most ears lacks the elegance, wit, charm and simplicity of the original.

And their endline, 'Change your words. Change your world' feels exactly like that: the end of a video designed to promote an agency, produce clicks and self-consciously garner attention. Somewhere the innocence has gone missing.

B) WHY THEY SAID IT

The agency then also had to admit that theirs was a homage to an earlier film, by Alonso Alvarez Barredo, *Historia de un Letrero (The Story of a Sign)*. This 5-minute short film won an award in 2008. But going even further back in social media epochal terms, a creative called Nick Galanides produced a virtually identical video four years earlier. Which just goes to show you can't keep an old re-plagiarized idea down.

An anecdote relating to Monty Python's John Cleese: According to the tale, Cleese was making a TV ad/trailer for the BBC in 1986 encouraging people to pay their TV licence fee, the way in which the BBC has historically been funded. The ad was a re-purposing of a scene from Life of Brian (1979), generally referred to as 'what have the Romans ever done for us?' in order to demonstrate the breadth of programmes and channels offered by the BBC in return for the license fee.

In the scene in Brian, the People's Front of Judaea are having a factional row with the Judaean People's Front, a satire on the bickering and internecine rivalries among the likes of trade unionists and guerrilla organizations. The movements appear to spend more time fighting among themselves than against the Romans.

When meeting the creative team who had created the ad/trailer for the BBC TV license campaign, Cleese was said to have responded: "Ah, so it takes two people to steal an idea does it?"

C) WHEN YOU SHOULD USE IT

- Ideally, hardly ever carry out an exact remake, except as a cautionary tale about the diminishing returns of remakes (aka the Law of *Speed 2*)

- Or a faintly glib reminder that words change the world (which sounds only marginally less trivial when paraphrased)

- But also, as a warning to make sure that you check what you are told/given: there may be hidden history which betrays a completely different set of facts

TAGS: advertising, myth, storytelling, simplicity

16. "GNOTHI SEAUTON"

WHO SAID IT AND IN WHAT CONTEXT

Delphi was home to the oracle of Apollo, one of the most venerated places in the whole of Greece and one of the few things all Greeks could agree and converge on.

As well as a sacred sanctuary and home to the 'omphalos' (literally 'navel'), which the Greeks thought was the centre of the universe, it was the home of the Panhellenic games every four years. The Greeks believed that Zeus sent two eagles from opposite ends of the world to determine the centre of the world, and where they crossed would be that place.

The stone is still visible today and there is an omphalos in the Church of the Holy Sepulchre in Jerusalem.

People woud come from across Greece (Hellas as it was known) to ask the priestess of Apollo, the Pythia, for oracular advice. One who sought such answers was King Croesus, legendarily wealthy King of Lydia. He asked the oracle whether he should wage war with Persia. He was told – not yet, that would have been too simple – that if he did, he would destroy a great empire. Croesus took this as the equivalent of a UN resolution and went to war, only to be utterly defeated. It would be his own empire that would be crushed.

The oracle often gave what appeared at first sight to be tantalizingly positive advice only to have the last laugh: one nil to the Pythia.

(The Greeks were suckers for enigma and irony. Ask Oedipus.)

A slightly more positive piece of ambiguity greeted Athenian leader Themistocles when he asked how to defend Athens against the superior military might of Xerxes, King of Persia in 480 BCE. A second oracle pronounced that only a 'wooden wall' would save Athens. Themistocles took this as validation to build a naval fleet of unprecedented strength. This he did, and Athens used it to win a spectacular naval battle at Salamis. Themistocles interpreted the wooden wall as meaning the Athenian navy.

Now, carved on the forecourt at Delphi were three maxims.

The first and most famous was *gnothi seauton*, 'know yourself'. The second was *meden agan*, 'nothing in excess' because the Greeks tended to rail against ostentatious excess, seeing it as the characteristic behaviour of foreigners or barbarians. The third remains rather ambiguous.

B) WHY THEY SAID IT

If Delphi were a brand, 'know yourself' would be its tagline.

The origin of the maxim is uncertain (as you might expect from the home of an oracle). But they were seen as universally useful advice from a culture that revered moderation (hence 'nothing in excess').

In the same way 'know yourself' was partly an injunction against hubris, unchecked pride and arrogance, though in modern times it has perhaps been over-interpreted in a more contemporary psychology-of-self-awareness-sense.

Just as Socrates later proclaimed that, "The unexamined life is not worth living", the advice from the temple was to understand the role of mankind and one's own limits.

C) WHEN YOU SHOULD USE IT

Predictably it has been echoed and adapted in modern culture. Famously, the cultural mishmash that was the film series *The Matrix* borrowed the wisdom of the ancients. One character, literally The Oracle, had the words *temet nosce* – know yourself – over the door (the Latin presumably marginally less obscure to a popcorn-munching audience than the Greek).

- Our era is characterized by the need or drive for self-discovery, but where should we look for answers?

- As we saw with Number 1, not everyone thinks 'knowing oneself' is a worthwhile mission. From Oscar Wilde who believed rather impudently that "Only the shallow know themselves" to many modern thinkers who feel the obsession with 'knowing who we are' or becoming who we are flies in the face of reality, some feel that we cannot truly know ourselves in a single, unchanging 'essentialist' sense

- But, perhaps, knowing that we are amenable to internal factors, and contexts of which we remain unaware and susceptible to ambivalence and inconsistency, shouldn't get in the way of trying to understand ourselves a little better

TAGS: behaviour, maxims, classics

17. POVS ...

A) WHO SAID IT AND IN WHAT CONTEXT

First, a disclaimer. My company name is POV, as in point of view. I chose it because it reflects two things I believed in or had meaning for me: firstly, as a refugee from the advertising industry, I had been used to seeing scripts from creative people using 'pov' to denote a copywriting or screenwriting convention that we see something from this character's point of view.

Secondly, I also wanted something that could act as a manifesto to argue that in work, in education, in business and branding we need to actively seek to not withhold a point of view: character, personality, direction – all things that what I termed the arithmocracy (a system obsessed with measurement, numbers and metrics) was in danger of anathematizing.

So, at one level, the answer to who said it in this case is 'me'.

But the pov has other meanings, and one I want to focus on is ... 'popular orange vegetable'. Yes, a synonym for carrot.

It is an in-joke at the UK-based newspaper and online news source *The Guardian* (but more than that) after one of their journalists, Jamie Fahey, spotted the phrase and removed the manifestly drab synonym from a draft piece in the *Liverpool Echo*. They define a pov as:

> *"Term coined by a* Guardian *journalist to depict laboured attempts to produce synonyms by writers seeking what H.W. Fowler called 'elegant variation' (and Orwell 'inelegant variation'), often descending into cliché or absurdity. Thus, Dalí becomes 'the moustachioed surrealist".*

B) WHY THEY SAID IT

So, the 'extraneous, tautologous and invasive' phrase becomes a creative way of avoiding clunky repetition or resorting to repeating rather lifeless pronouns like 'it' or 'they'. Some povs are delightfully eccentric, some bizarre: Ireland being described as the 'cockatoo-shaped landmass' on BBC Radio 4 takes some beating. Another more antiquated US source characterizes the vegetarian as 'the confirmed spinach-addict' or describes eggnog as the 'creamy holiday beverage' or in the *New York Herald Tribune*, a beaver was almost known incognito as 'the furry, paddle-tailed mammal'.

Perhaps the discoverer's rights belong with US journalist Charles W. Morton. He spotted a pov in the *Boston Transcript* in the 1930s, where a banana was referred to as 'an elongated yellow fruit' in a story about some fugitive monkeys and the efforts of local law enforcement to recover them using said bright incentive, to no great advantage.

Morton explained in *A Slight Sense of Outrage* (1955):

> *"It does bespeak an author who wishes to appear witty, knowledgeable and versatile … it can also bespeak an author who is merely pompous."*

The objection is that by and large they are unnecessary, usually longer synonyms for a simple, concise noun or pronoun, as the 'stroppy editor' website advised in a 2013 blogpost against them.

C) WHEN YOU SHOULD USE IT

- In the fight against meaningless jargon, I obviously side with those who trumpet the need for simplicity and elegance over ambiguity. Call a banana a banana, a spade a spade. Brexit, it appears, means Brexit

- But hold on. If we want to become more creative, more curious and more playful at work, why not use the pov as a challenge?

- Is the same word better than lame repetition? Shouldn't we also try to exercise our creativity to avoid serial repetition of the same word?

TAGS: language, creativity, curiosity, humour

18. "ENTIA NON SUNT MULTIPLICANDA PRAETER NECESSITATEM"

A) WHO SAID IT AND IN WHAT CONTEXT

These days Occam's (or Ockham's) razor would in all likelihood be something Gerard Butler would be found advertising, and Occam would be a YouTube influencer working for a global communications agency. But his influence would abide nonetheless.

For 14th century Franciscan monk, William of Occam (or Ockham) is alleged to have said something that has rung down the ages, *"Entia non sunt multiplicanda praeter necessitatem."*

Or, translated from the Latin, things should not be multiplied beyond the necessary, otherwise known as the principle of parsimony. Although associated with William, the thinking goes back to Aquinas and before that to Aristotle.

The razor refers to the shaving away of anything unnecessary. Occam is suggesting that theories are meant to do things, that is to explain and predict, and this can be accomplished more effectively with as few assumptions as are needed.

Subsequently, many scientists have adopted or adapted Occam's razor: German polymath Gottfried Leibniz (1646-1716) spoke of 'identity of observables' and Isaac Newton stated the rule: "We are to admit no more causes of natural things than such as are both true and sufficient to explain their appearances. For nature is pleased with simplicity."

In *A Brief History of Time*, Stephen Hawking attributed the discovery of quantum physics to the application of Occam's razor.

B) WHY THEY SAID IT

William was a believer in 'fideism', where belief in God is at heart a matter of faith rather than knowledge. As such, his principle of simplicity derived from a sense that divine omnipotence makes everything as simple as it can be.

Or consider an equation and possibly the most celebrated and T-shirtable one of them all: Einstein's e=mc^2.

An extraordinary amount of information, history and all-round standing on the shoulders of giants is contained within that miniscule nugget. And a nugget that so few of us can actually then decode and pass on with any sense of confidence.

C) WHEN YOU SHOULD USE IT

- At its simplest (as it were), Occam's theory advocates simplicity in order to reduce the risk of error. Every hypothesis carries within it the possibility that it may be wrong, so the more hypotheses one accepts, the higher the risk of error

- But maybe we need to counterbalance Occam with Einstein, who allegedly claimed: *"Everything should be made as simple as possible, but not simpler"*

- So, we need to recognize the power of those who trumpet the need for simplicity and prioritise elegance over ambiguity

- We also need to be aware that nature – for all its love of simplicity – also adores redundancy. Darwin showed that nature is often redundant in form and function

TAGS: science, simplicity

19. "ECONOMICAL WITH THE TRUTH"

WHO SAID IT AND IN WHAT CONTEXT

An occasional pastime I can recommend is grubbing around for the latest ways in which people avoid using the term 'lie'.

In the British Parliament the custom is to employ the phrase 'to mislead the House'. As long ago as 1906 Winston Churchill coined the term 'terminological inexactitude' as a way of euphemistically suggesting a member of parliament was lying.

More recently the word 'disingenuous' appears to have stepped into the breach. The cross-examining of James Murdoch in connection with the *News of the World* phone hacking scandal in 2010-2012, as is the case with most high-profile legal cases, threw up some interesting gobbets of evasiveness:

- 'It predated my involvement'
- 'I don't recall'
- 'I'm not aware of it'

- 'To my knowledge/as I understand it'
- 'I can find no record'

But perhaps the granddaddy of them all was the use of 'economical with the truth', spoken by then British Cabinet Secretary, Robert Armstrong, during the Australian 'Spycatcher' trial of former MI5 assistant director, Peter Wright, in 1986.

Wright had published his memoirs in Australia, *Spycatcher: The Candid Autobiography of a Senior Intelligence Officer*, which the British Government sought to ban. In it, Wright had made some scandalously juicy allegations.

B) WHY THEY SAID IT

'Economical with the truth' was recorded as far back as the 18th century from the mouth of Edmund Burke, the Irish statesman and thinker, although rarely used since. Mark Twain also (predictably) had his version, "Truth is the most valuable thing we have. Let us economize it."

It was brought into the contemporary language by Armstrong, when questioned by Aussie lawyer – and later Prime Minister – Malcolm Turnbull. (At the time, Turnbull was a brash young arriviste, known afterwards as the 'cocky pom-basher' but also in a feat of nominative determinism was known to 'turn bullish'. "He's a prick," said an ex-business-partner, when asked to describe Turnbull, who claimed he "was being restrained in what he says so as not to fuel an ongoing feud".

The Spycatcher exchange has now gone down in legal, political and memetic folklore:

Turnbull: What is the difference between a mislead-
            ing impression and a lie?
Armstrong: A lie is a straight untruth.
Turnbull: What is a misleading impression – a sort
            of bent untruth?
Armstrong: As one person said, it is perhaps being
            'economical with the truth'.

In 1992, Aaron Sorkin would put Tom Cruise into a similar situation to needle Jack Nicholson in *A Few Good Men*, facing him down that "you can't handle the truth".

By forcing Armstrong to admit the British Government was prepared to lie to protect national interests and use prevarication and sophistry in the face of unvarnished Aussie brashness and honesty, Turnbull effectively won the battle in that exchange. And the book, eventually, was published.

In 1992, the phrase returned to short-term prominence. Tory Minister for Trade, Alan Clark was cross-examined during the 'arms to Iraq' case when the machine tools manufacturer Matrix Churchill was accused of illegally selling arms to Saddam Hussein during the Iraq war, and Clark added his own embellishment to the phrase.

As Minister for Trade under Margaret Thatcher, he was effectively admitting the government's complicity.

> Clark: *Well it's our old friend 'being economical',*
> *isn't it?*
> Lawyer: *With the truth?*
> Clark: *With the actualité*

c) WHEN YOU SHOULD USE IT

- There are times when a well-turned phrase is always welcome, especially if one has to admit to failure or inaccuracy, or one has to accuse a co-worker of similar

- These expressions, although admittedly evasive and weaselly, might still be welcome as way of opening up a more diplomatic or light-touch approach

TAGS: simplicity, communication

20. THE STANFORD PRISON EXPERIMENT AND THE FAE

The Lucifer Effect, written by Stanford psychologist Philip Zimbardo, is a story of two famous cases. This work is an in-depth analysis of the causes of evil and how we are culturally driven to elevate dispositional explanations of human behaviour over the situational: that is, we tend to blame people's character for their behaviour rather than the contextual factors that may not be as immediately apparent to us.

Much of the book is devoted to the Stanford Prison Experiment (SPE) of 1971. Often recreated for TV specials and relentlessly discussed ever since even beyond the narrow academic sphere, it is still shocking and exhilarating to read of how an experiment using a disparate group of bright, middle-class students in Palo Alto, California, turned into a shocking display and dissection of human evil. To such an extent, in fact, that Zimbardo had to terminate it prematurely after only six days.

B) WHY THEY SAID IT

Twenty-four undergraduates were chosen to play the roles of either guards or prisoners and live in a mock prison in the basement of the Stanford psychology building for two weeks. Those selected were chosen precisely because they had no obvious psychological issues or criminal history. To randomize the selection further, the roles of prisoner and guard were allocated solely on the toss of a coin.

In graphic detail over nearly 250 pages of densely-packed but elegantly written prose, Zimbardo takes us through the chronology, implications, meanings and messages of the SPE. This is a demonstration of what is called the 'fundamental attribution error' (FAE), where we tend to naturally over-estimate the role of character at the expense of context.

The second part of the book is based on the Abu Ghraib prison in Iraq. It made global headlines in 2004 when photographs of US military personnel abusing Iraqi prisoners flashed round the world. The similarities with the SPE were obvious and Zimbardo outlined the case for a general theory of human nature, and the pathway to evil, based on his inter-pretation both of the SPE and the special set of cir-cumstance and the broader context that led to Abu Ghraib. Seven soldiers were convicted and two were sentenced to imprisonment.

Zimbardo was called as an expert witness at the trial of the US soldiers. He argued that their actions were the tragic result of perceived anonymity, the absence of a sense of personal responsibility, and tacit approval by military commanders, factors that had been shown in experiments to make good people do evil.

Zimbardo to this day attempts to highlight what he sees as a crucial difference between the 'bad apple' effect and the 'bad barrel' view.

In the first (bad apple), it is too easy to assume that a rogue student-jailer or an Abu Ghraib soldier is a bad apple, that is a one-off example of pure evil.

What Zimbardo argues is that we must look more closely at the effect of the 'bad barrel', in other words what context does or can do to the individual and group. In more technical terms, this is called 'dispositional psychology'.

C) WHEN YOU SHOULD USE IT

- One of the most significant implications to be drawn from his thinking is to suggest that we need to remember how quixotic we all are as human beings. We are not always (in fact very rarely are) predictable

- The moral of *The Lucifer Effect* is that often context will override behaviour and content. Zimbardo asks us to consider the possibility that "each of us has the potential or mental templates, to be saint or sinner, altruistic or selfish, gentle or cruel"

- Perhaps, he argues, we are born with a variety of capacities, each of which is activated and developed depending on the social and cultural circumstances that govern our lives

- At the very least, we need to pull back and not just look at human behaviour and causality from the point of view of the individual and their nexus of values, beliefs and attitudes. The 'dispositional view' directs us to also look out for the barrels (the specific context of 'consumer behaviour') and the barrel makers, people who are responsible for creating the context in question

- As long as we cling on to the notion that there is an essential, unchanging character inherent in people (in the SPE terms, that they are not and never can be 'evil'), we will carry out segmentation studies and other analysis which tries to pigeonhole and compartmentalize people into rigid segments

- And we may treat out family, friends and colleagues differently if we force ourselves to take a less dispositional perspective

TAGS: behavioural economics, acronym

21. "WE ARE INSECURE, PRAISE-STARVED FLATTERY SLUTS"

A) WHO SAID IT AND IN WHAT CONTEXT

The anthropologist Mary Douglas was exerting a profound effect on marketing and brand thinkers of the 1970s and 1980s. Her analysis laid the foundations for a new humanistic view of the brand as a totem within a tribe or community rather than merely a collection of product benefits and messages.

Evolutionary psychologists have made their discipline quite cool over recent years, as new insights began to arrive in the mainstream, and writers such as Steven Pinker (see Number 13), Matt Ridley, David Buss, Randy Nesse, Robert Wright, and Tooby and Cosmides drew the sting from earlier sociobiology from the likes of E. O. Wilson and the work of Trivers, Hamilton and Dawkins in developing the new Darwinian synthesis. It wasn't all one-way for Evo Psycho as many critics claimed that their theories were unprovable 'just-so stories'.

One of the more enduring and insightful exponents is Geoffrey Miller. This may be at least partly to do with his interest in the application of evolutionary psychology to consumerism, in search of what might almost be described as a fundamental theory of consumer behaviour.

In *Spent*, he explores how the consumer and marketing mindset is intimately bound up with our inherent instincts from our earliest forefathers to signal our social status in order to maximize reproductive success. Signalling theory for Miller is one of the great revolutions in thinking in recent decades.

Central to this is how sexual selection through mate choice might have shaped human mental evolution using marketing metaphors: males used sales tactics to seduce sceptical female customers into accepting free trials of their FMCG (fast-moving-consumer-goods: aka sperm, which are certainly pretty f-m).

B) WHY THEY SAID IT

According to this fiercely direct blend of marketing savvy and evolutionary psychology, our brains have a deep and hard-wired drive to succeed in two major evolutionary goals: displaying fitness indicators that were associated with higher social and sexual status in prehistory and chasing fitness cues.

Where Miller differs from many brand experts (and practitioners) is his insistence that display overrides consumption as it is more driven by the public display of status, rather than consumption being focused on a private desire for personal pleasure and therefore not manifested.

"A brand in this world is merely a tool for impression management and a means of performing strategic trait signalling."

This does not necessarily paint an especially glamorous picture of the human condition. Miller appreciates that this 'will to display' makes us "insecure, praise-starved flattery sluts".

Now that's what I call a T-shirt. Money, therefore, is a form of 'liquid fitness'.

c) WHEN YOU SHOULD USE IT

As a result, Miller argues manufacturers "still believe that premium products are bought to display wealth, status and taste, and they miss the deeper mental traits that people are actually wired to display – traits such as kindness, intelligence and creativity". This, Miller claims, limits their success rate.

- Miller famously had a very unusual take on ethnography: his most famous paper relied on observing lap dancers in order to understand male sexual psychology. So, maybe we all need to emulate his approach and think more laterally about how to design experiments to generate insight

- If Miller is right, the communications world needs to worry less about displaying wealth and status and more on subtle traits such as kindness, intelligence, creativity and personality. Again, this might be a lesson we can learn and thus worry less about what clients think they are selling and more on what it is people are buying

- In Miller's words, much of human behaviour, whether consumption or charity, is engendered by motives of costly signalling to display our personal qualities to potential mates and other social partners

- Another lesson is that we need to build more bridges between the world of academia – where the likes of Miller operate – and practitioners who are on the front line of working with brands and consumers

TAGS: behaviour, communication

2. "A HOLY TERROR OF CHANCE"

A) WHO SAID IT AND IN WHAT CONTEXT

"Men cannot conceive that things occur by chance ... they have a holy terror of chance." (cited by Stephen Jay Gould in *Conversations About the End of Time*).

It seems like a bygone age with fear and superstition, but as the new millennium approached there were deep-seated fears of a practical – the Y2K bug and planes falling out of the sky – and spiritual kind – was the end of the world indeed nigh? In retrospect, evidence increasingly suggests not.

Speaking to French journalists, four great thinkers from the worlds of science and the arts gathered to ponder the big questions underlying those fears. Novelist, mediaevalist and semiotician Umberto Eco, palaeontologist Stephen Jay Gould, screenwriter Jean-Claude Carrière and Catholic historian Jean Delumeau all deliberated the role and nature of time through history, covering concepts of millenarianism, cyberspace, slowness and the apocalypse.

B) WHY THEY SAID IT

Many scientists have come to define our species as 'pattern-makers'.

Take the Nobel laureate, physicist and Santa Fe complexity guru, Murray Gell-Mann, the man who coined the word 'quark' after a passage in Joyce. In *The Quark and the Jaguar* he talks of people as being Complex Adaptive Systems (CAS).

In this way, he believes, there are universal similarities among some of the most crucial processes on Earth: biological evolution, ecological systems, the mammalian immune system, the evolution of human societies and sophisticated computer software systems, to name but a few.

Each of these processes rely on gathering information about itself and its interactions with the environment, building a model based on the regularities it perceives. So, in the case of human individuals, we think, learn, use symbolic language and generate new generations of CASs in our wake. Later, he adapts the term CAS to include interpreter and observer of the information: this he calls an Information Gathering and Utilizing System (IGUS).

According to this thinking, through both our biological inheritance and our culture, we are primed to seek patterns. The desire to link all things together goes back as far as Pythagoras and his number-gods and the harmony of the spheres. Patterns work as editing devices, maps of a world too complex, chaotic and swollen with information for us to survive. Our minds seek out patterns in order to let us expand our mental powers and move on to higher planes.

At times this pattern-seeking can lead us astray, trying desperately to impose order where there is none. This, perhaps, explains the attractions of pastimes like astrology, the ink-blot test and certain types of modern art.

"Symbolic interpretation is interpreted because we refuse to accept that any input is meaningless. Shown an inkblot we see witches, bats and dragons. This refusal to accept that input is noise lies at the root of divination by tarot cards, tea leaves ...", John Maynard Smith *The Theory of Evolution* 1993, cited in Calvin's *The Cerebral Code*, 1996.

c) WHEN YOU SHOULD USE IT

- Too often when we are looking for explanations we rely on our pattern-seeking brain to give us simple, causal links

- But the Eco quote reminds us that we need to be alert to these unconscious processes and give chance its fair say in understanding how things happen and not give in to our 'holy terror of chance'

- What Michael Shermer terms 'agenticity' is another way of appreciating that we naturally want to ascribe actions to an agent (either human or divine), when we need to accept this might be the desire of our brains to look for a meaningful pattern or causal relationship where there is none

TAGS: causality, unconscious

23. "WE REWEAVE, RATHER THAN RETRIEVE"

A) WHO SAID IT AND IN WHAT CONTEXT

As we saw earlier (Number 12), in *Stumbling on Happiness*, Harvard psychology professor and TED Talks star, Daniel Gilbert, discusses some of the weaknesses of our thinking systems and our inability to forecast our emotional states.

He also shows how the brain creates illusions to fill in gaps, and how 'the elaborate tapestry of our experience' is not stored in its entirety but is compressed. So that later when we want to recall that experience our brains "reweave the tapestry by fabricating, not by actually retrieving" the bulk of information.

This is the conclusion of much new work into how memory works in the last few years, especially in the now hectically busy domain of consciousness studies. So, Tor Nørretranders in *The User Illusion* (book-jacketed rather dismissively as 'Denmark's leading science writer') cites Joseph LeDoux:

"Weaving such tales about the self and its world is a prime function of consciousness."

B) WHY THEY SAID IT

"Historians constantly rewrite history, reinterpreting (reorganizing) the records of the past. So, too, when the brain's coherent responses become a part of a memory, they are organized anew as part of the structure of consciousness. What makes them memories is that they become part of that structure and thus form part of the sense of self."

Israel Rosenfield, *The Strange, Familiar and Forgotten: An Anatomy of Consciousness*

Equally, in the words of the late British psychologist Stuart Sutherland's vastly underrated *Irrationality*, we remember what we expect to hear.

Scientists have gathered much evidence (again, crucially, from literature as well as science) to conclude that we should stop thinking of remembering as a passive process of calling up a stored fact and printing it out. Rather than merely pulling a document from file manager, we should return to the etymology of 'remember', with its implication of 'assembling', 'connecting' and active participation in the process.

In *Private Myths: Dreams and Dreaming*, the Jungian analyst Anthony Stevens attempts to review dream interpretation in the light of modern neuroscience and shows how it might be possible to regard dreams in a more biological light, rescuing them from the sexual arena of Freud. In so doing, he quotes the Cambridge psychologist Sir Frederic Bartlett, from his 1932 work *Remembering*:

"Remembering is not the re-excitation of innumerable, fixed lifeless and fragmentary traces: it is imaginative reconstruction, built out of the attitude of our relation toward a whole mass of organized past reactions or experiences. An active, dynamic process which like perceiving, imagining and recognizing is based on past experience but takes account of the current situation and needs."

C) WHEN YOU SHOULD USE IT

- More salutary advice about the taken-for-granted. We all think it natural, don't we, to imagine that the computer metaphor holds for our brains: so, we put a document in a folder, we pick it out (retrieve) and lo! It is unchanged

- But the evidence from the neuroscientists and other specialists into memory seems irrevocable: that the brain with its drive toward plasticity is constantly reconstructing our memories (and to some extent, therefore, our 'selves') and that imagination has a far greater impact on the process of remembering than we wish were the case

TAGS: myths, memory, brain

24. "HYPOTHESES ARE ADVENTURES OF THE MIND"

A) WHO SAID IT AND IN WHAT CONTEXT

Peter Medawar (1915-1987) was considered one of the most prominent scientists of his generation, a biologist whose work in immunology earned him the sobriquet of 'the father of transplantation' and the Nobel prize in 1960.

He was also lauded as a brilliant communicator, author and wit: Richard Dawkins began the entry on Medawar in *The Oxford Book of Modern Science Writing* with "... he is surely the wittiest of all science writers."

As an indication, I give you his lacerating comment from a 1961 review of Pierre Teilhard de Chardin's *The Phenomenon of Man*:

"Its author can be excused of dishonesty only on the grounds that before deceiving others he has taken great pains to deceive himself."

In *The Art of the Soluble* he added elegantly:

"Scientists have dull lives: if a scientist were to cut his ear off, no one would take it as a sign of heightened sensibility."

But here let us focus on and admire his declaration:

"Hypotheses are adventures of the mind."

B) WHY THEY SAID IT

One of his most popular books was on the topic of philosophy of science, *The Art of The Soluble*, which was later chosen as his most life-changing book by neuroscientist V. S. Ramachandran. In that work, he declared that if – as was commonly stated politics was the art of the possible – for Medawar science was the art of the soluble:

"Good scientists study the most important problems they think they can solve. It is, after all, their professional business to solve problems not to grapple with them."

But look more closely at the subheading: 'creativity and originality in science'.

Medawar defined creativity as *"a faculty of mind or spirit that empowers us to bring into existence, ostensibly out of nothing, something of beauty, order or significance".*

Medawar endorsed the view that creativity can be broader than the commonly accepted definition and is by no means unscientific, when he said:

"Designing a hypothesis is a creative act in the sense that it is the invention of a possible world, or a possible fragment of a world."

He cites French physiologist Claude Bernard 1865:

"To experiment without a preconceived idea is to wander aimlessly."

c) WHEN YOU SHOULD USE IT

- For Medawar, scientists are problem-seekers as much as solvers. Science is essentially a biological compulsion, the hunter-feeling. He felt that a good scientist was – in another memorable expression – discovery-prone

- Creativity was very much part of the scientific enterprise. For Medawar the bold use of imagination was the rule in scientific discoveries, not the exception. Hypotheses arise from inspiration

- So, we must conclude that any fake compartmentalization of science and art (where one is creative, the other administratively functional) is false: scientists use the same hypothetical, creative processes as their arts-based colleagues

- Let us all look to hypotheses as more than just dry and dusty equations for people in lab coats: they are the essence of creativity and originality

- For those of us operating within the domain of communications and research, this discussion brings to mind the words of Alan Hedges in his seminal (which for some of us is a euphemism for 'neglected') treatise on advertising development and testing, *Testing to Destruction*, first published in 1974. Hedges insisted on the need for creativity and science to be compatible bedfellows and to allow creativity to be never fully on the leash of measurement and quantification

TAGS: science, creativity

25. EATS, SHOOTS AND LEAVES – THE OXFORD COMMA

A) WHO SAID IT AND IN WHAT CONTEXT

One of the most unexpected publishing successes in recent times was Lynne Truss's *Eats, Shoots and Leaves: The Zero Tolerance Approach to Punctuation*, her polemic on punctuation based on a BBC Radio series she presented called *Cutting a Dash*. A novelist and dramatist besides, her contentious broadside against linguistic flabbiness created shockwaves that stunned even her publisher, who famously responded to the question of why it was so popular by remarking that *"it sold well because lots of people bought it"*.

Truss's publisher was (probably inadvertently) referring to a power law – the rich get richer effect, labelled 'cumulative advantage' by Duncan Watts, creator of the 'six degrees of separation' and renowned for his work in small world theory. This is not dissimilar to the so-called 'butterfly effect' and the power of tiny fluctuations in an initial condition to create disproportionately large changes in final outcomes.

In 'Eats, Shoots …', one of Truss's diatribes is in defence of the Oxford comma (also known as the serial or Harvard comma) because it was part of the Oxford University Press style guide for over a century. It is a comma used after the penultimate item in a list and before the conjunction for the avoidance of ambiguity.

B) WHY THEY SAID IT

The title of her book is based on the following joke:

> *A panda walks into a café. He orders a sandwich, eats it, then draws a gun and proceeds to fire it at the other patrons. 'Why?' asks the confused, surviving waiter amidst the carnage, as the panda makes toward the exit. The panda produces a badly punctuated wildlife manual and tosses it over his shoulder. 'Well, I'm a panda,' he says, at the door. 'Read the manual.' The waiter turns to the relevant entry in the manual and, sure enough, finds an explanation.*
>
> *'Panda. Large black-and-white bear-like mammal, native to China. Eats, shoots and leaves.'*

Her no-nonsense approach can also be typified by her pitiless verdict on the 'grocer's apostrophe':

> *"No matter that you have a PhD and have read all of Henry James twice. If you still persist in writing, 'Good food at it's best', you deserve to be struck by lightning, hacked up on the spot and buried in an unmarked grave."*

The role of the Oxford comma is one of Truss's targets, and why its staunchest exponents fight so vigorously in its defence is that it is one of the many tools available to aid grammatical intelligibility. It has even been cited in legal cases where clarity has become obfuscated.

Where the fun starts is where the absence of the Oxford comma creates ambiguity.

The Oxford comma – of course, it has its own Twitter existence – itself mentions two famous (but possibly apocryphal) examples.

- *'Among those interviewed were Merle Haggard's two ex-wives, Kris Kristofferson and Robert Duvall'*

- *This book is dedicated to my parents, Ayn Rand and God*

c) WHEN YOU SHOULD USE IT

- Clarity and simplicity are all. Whatever tools, techniques and assistance we can bring to aid those noble goals should be embraced with open arms (and brackets)

- The Oxford comma is a symbol of the fight for transparency and the 'grammar wars' are best seen as a struggle to ensure that we are all on the same side however much or little we obsess about grammatical pedantry

- Sometimes, technical, scientific or grammatical jargon is designed to bewitch, bother and bewilder; but sometimes, as with the Oxford comma, it should be enlisted on the side of simplicity and clarity

TAGS: clarity, communication, language

16. "FOR SALE. BABY SHOES"

A) WHO SAID IT AND IN WHAT CONTEXT

As myth and anecdote dipped in memory would have it, Ernest Hemingway was lunching at Luchow's, a celebrated East Village restaurant, famously associated with the legend *'Through the doors of Luchow's pass all the famous people of the world.'*

Hemingway was surrounded by a number of other writers and on this occasion proclaimed that he could write an entire short story that was only six words long. Hemingway told each of them to put ten dollars in the middle of the table; if he was wrong, he said, he'd match it. If he was right, he would keep the entire pot. He quickly wrote six words down on a napkin and passed it around; Papa, as Hemingway liked to name himself, won the bet.

The words were 'FOR SALE, BABY SHOES, NEVER WORN.' Voila, a beginning, a middle and an end and a myth was born.

In this telling, all the diners accepted this verdict as Hemingway smirked and scooped up the cash.

B) WHY THEY SAID IT

Except. In the same way that 'I'm blind ...' (see Number 14 – "I'm blind, please help") turns out to be a nugget of truth buried beneath several layers of myth, so does 'baby shoes'.

Perpetuated by many, the first link to Hemingway originated in 1992 from the Canadian literary figure John Robert Colombo. He printed part of a letter that he had received from the famous science fiction author Arthur C. Clarke, suggesting the story belonged to the 1920s. The combination of gruff writer and science fiction guru may have been enough to spread the story.

But it appears to have a history that predates Hemingway.

The 16 May 1910 edition of *The Spokane Press* included an article titled 'Tragedy of Baby's Death is Revealed in Sale of Clothes'.

As far back as 1927 there is evidence of a comic strip featuring the character Ella Cinders describing an advert for a baby carriage rather than shoes: the comic strip itself had been designed to encourage people to use the classified ads.

'THEY SAY THE GREATEST SHORT STORY IN THE WORLD WAS WRITTEN IN A SEVEN-WORD CLASSIFIED AD: "FOR SALE, A BABY CARRIAGE; NEVER USED!"

C) WHEN YOU SHOULD USE IT

- Stories and deeds of heroism tend to accrete around known idols. Hence Hemingway would be a more than suitable vehicle for the creation of this token of flash fiction. So, we must apply scepticism to our tendency of credulously assuming anecdote as created by a known giant

- Flash fiction itself is somewhat nebulous. According to the Bridport Prize, an international creative writing competition sponsored by the Bridport Arts Centre in Dorset, you can have a drabble (under 100) words or a dribble (under 50): the flash fiction website cites 'one-word stories' by Richard Kostelanetz, though most are more like a visual poem

- But with the arrival of a medium constraining its users to, at first, 140 and then 280 characters, 'twitterature' has been a positive force in driving conciseness and simplicity, and occasionally even literary merit

TAGS: language, sayings, myths, storytelling

27. "WITH IT OR ON IT …"

A) WHO SAID IT AND IN WHAT CONTEXT

Or … ἢ τὰν ἢ ἐπί τᾶς in the original Greek.

But you can also see it uttered by Gorgo (played by Lena Headey, aka *Game of Thrones* Cersei Lannister) to Gerard Butler's King Leonidas in Zach Snyder's movie *300* (2006), his rendition of the comic book series telling the story of the Battle of Thermopylae in 480 BCE, as the Greeks repelled the Persian invasion.

Born of a wealthy family in Boeotia, Greece around AD 46, Plutarch was a biographer and essayist most famed for his *Parallel Lives*, a series of paired biographies – one Greek and one Roman. He later received Roman citizenship.

His *Ethika* in Greek (*Moralia*, in Latin, or morals, ethics) was a loosely assembled and eclectic collection of essays and speeches.

In a section called 'Sayings of Spartan Women' (*Moralia 241*), he quotes various sayings of women of that Greek state. The one that concerns us here is,

"Another, as she handed her son his shield, exhorted him, saying, 'Either (with) this or upon this'."

Unlike most other parts of Greece where women were very much second-class citizens, in Sparta (perhaps surprisingly) they could own property and take part in many other civic duties. When asked by a traveller from another part of Greece, why Spartan women seemed to be allowed to rule their men, Gorgo (again) responds, *"Because we are the only ones who give birth to them."*

B) WHY THEY SAID IT

This seems to refer to a custom which, even though Plutarch was writing perhaps 300 years after the heyday of the Spartan warrior culture he describes, seems to have been in line with the common conception of Spartan culture.

Spartan mothers, in particular, come out in Plutarch as peculiarly hard-hearted and stoic in the cause of the greater Spartan good: namely, Spartan victory.

C) WHEN YOU SHOULD USE IT

- Do you ever think you should be more 'laconic'? If so, you are trying to be more Spartan – an adjective commonly used to suggest something austere, harsh, unadorned, frugal and perhaps uncomfortable

- But we now use the word laconic to mean dry, understated or biting wit: this was often in contrast to Attic wit – more sophisticated and dazzling by contrast, and derived from Greece's cosmopolitan and cultural epicentre, Athens and its environs. Laconic comes from the area of Laconia, which included Sparta (in the classical age they were known as Lakedaimonioi not Spartans)

- So, keep it simple and minimalist. There is something dry and even menacing about the Spartans' laconic responses. See also Number 61 below

- Though whether these deserve to be called Spartan catchphrases, (as warhistoryonline.com does) is open to debate

- GORGO is also the name of a brand (inevitably): an 'online fitness, nutrition and wellness resource for next level women'. Whether the allusion to Spartan women is welcome is one for conjecture or focus groups

28. "SUPERNATURAL CONTAGION" – IT'S A KIND OF MAGIC

A) WHO SAID IT AND IN WHAT CONTEXT

In his book, *Supersense*, British psychologist Bruce Hood explores the brain science of belief and narrates one of his most memorable/notorious experiments to elucidate the nature of disgust.

The book explores the existence and power of our 'supersense' – something which goes beyond reason and logic and allows us to infer the existence of patterns or forces.

Hood begins by dramatically showing off a pen: "It belonged to Albert Einstein," he tells a duly impressed audience. Everyone wants to hold it, to share in the reverence for this sacred tool. But this is just the warm-up.

He proceeds to hold up a tattered cardigan and asks if anyone would be happy to wear it. Most hands go up. He asks for volunteers to try on the jumper that he was holding up and offers a reward. At this point he adds one titbit of information – it belonged to the British serial killer Fred West.

At this point the natural feeling of disgust kicks in and the majority of subjects decline the financial incentive. Fear of contamination is too overpowering for a rational trade-off to be worthwhile. Morality trumps economics.

What is even more enlightening is the coda to the experiment (as is so often the case). Even when Hood reveals that it is not really a serial killer's knitwear, but a set-up, most still refuse his challenge. The contagion is too emotionally embedded to be swatted away with something like reality.

Hood suggests this is not a religious attitude to the supernatural, but merely an automatic, reflex supersense that gets in the way of us optimizing our rationality, a social glue that operates in the form of unconscious automatic shortcuts, known as heuristics.

(Hood credits Paul Rozin's work on disgust as the springboard for his stunt.)

Hood examined the degree of attachment that children have with objects, which demonstrate that we have an essentialist belief that there is something special about them. This is what he calls 'supernatural contagion', whereby we seem to be possessed of a desire to own or even touch items as though they are sacraments or reliquaries with invisible properties associated with significant individuals. By possessing them or having contact with them, and believing in invisible essences, we feel we can connect in some way with these objects of worship.

B) WHY THEY SAID IT

Analogous to this is the way that linguists talk of the concept of 'word magic'.

It covers a broad domain, from spells, incantations, prayers and curses to taboos and euphemisms; we all have the feeling that saying the very word can tempt the reality, even though most of our lives we act as mature materialists who can readily understand that the pairing of sound and meaning is arbitrary. It is arguably the same principle behind homeopathy (that 'like treats like').

C) WHEN YOU SHOULD USE IT

- Hood's supersense and supernatural contagion is another insightful way to see how we really behave. Disgust – both physical and moral – is far more influential in how we act and think than we like to admit. Much of what we believe is thoughtfully considered and grounded in a rational consideration of pros and cons, is in fact heavily influenced by emotions like moral disgust

- (Consider many hot topics – anything from abortion, climate change, same-sex marriages.)

- This is very much the placebo effect, whereby the mind is tricking the body. Arguably this should just be called the 'belief' effect rather than the 'placebo'

- Nor should we forget that this is also how brands operate. The brand as talisman will not work across all markets, clearly, but I think too many companies have been rather good at denying the belief-based, emotional and quasi-mystic ways in which brands work in this rather primitive and unconscious manner

TAGS: behavioural economics, brands, magic

29. "ALIEFS"

The term 'alief' was coined by Tamar Gendler, Professor of Philosophy and Psychology and Cognitive Sciences at Yale University.

Gendler was trying to highlight the distinction between our beliefs and something more primitive that underlies many of our less apparently rational decisions and reactions.

Paul Rozin's work with disgust (we saw him in Number 28 with 'supernatural contagion') is one area where Gendler posits the effect of aliefs: as Rozin's team demonstrated, if you take two pieces of fudge and mould one into the shape of a muffin and the other into a dog turd, even if you know that they are both fudge, an automatic and habitual override kicks in which presses the 'disgust' button.

Gendler, as well as others like Daniel Dennett and Paul Bloom (in *How Pleasure Works*), have embraced Gendler's concept and applied it in fields from the pleasure of storytelling, to the existence of supernatural and religious beliefs, and even to some mental disorders.

Going further back, the philosopher David Hume tells the story of a man who is hung out of a high tower in a cage of iron. He knows (rationally, he believes) that he is perfectly safe but, still, he 'cannot forebear trembling'.

Gendler describes the Grand Canyon Skywalk, the glass walkway that extends 70 feet from the rim of the canyon. It is considered to be such a draw for adrenaline junkies that many drive several miles over a dirt road to get there, only to find they are too afraid to step onto the walkway. In all of these cases, people know they are perfectly safe, the data is available and clear, but that doesn't stop them from feeling scared.

Or think about how people felt after Spielberg's film *Jaws* was released in 1975: beliefs tell cinema-goers it's a movie with a fake, plastic shark but your alief says 'don't go swimming in the sea – or in some cases – in a pool'.

B) WHY THEY SAID IT

For Gendler, beliefs are attitudes that we hold in response to how things are. Aliefs are more primitive. They are 'automatic and habitual belief-like attitudes', responses to how things instinctively *seem*. In the jargon to which philosophers and psychologists are so prone, they are 'affective, associative, automatic and arrational' (if this is a word): hence Gendler called them a-liefs. Presumably, also because 'a' precedes 'b' (as in belief).

The problem is when there is a disconnect between our beliefs and our aliefs, our aliefs remain stubbornly at work pulling the strings behind the scene.

Psychologist Paul Bloom extends the use of alief to the pleasures of the imagination; for Bloom, imagination is 'Reality Lite', "a useful substitute when the real pleasure is inaccessible, too risky, or too much work."

C) WHEN YOU SHOULD USE IT

- Gendler was not slow to use alief to explain why so many of our implicit biases drive our thoughts and actions, for example pervasive racism

- Gendler's term allows us to think that when we recoil in front of a turd-shaped item of confectionery or refuse to wear a murderer's jumper, we are not being irrational but susceptible to the powerful force that is our alief

- So, for example, in most public communication we are always being given information in an attempt to modify our beliefs, but it may be our stubborn, unconscious aliefs that really need working on

TAGS: behavioural economics, irrationality, neologism

30. "TOO MUCH INFORMATION"

WHO SAID IT AND IN WHAT CONTEXT

The first citation of 'too much information' (TMI) is credited to *Wall Street Journal* reporter Joseph Checkler around 1988.

There are now a quintillion articles (or thereabouts) on the internet on the subject of information overload on the internet, and we are all adrift in tiny bubbles on a sea of information. A Pew study in April 2016 of 1,520 Americans aged 18 and older showed (only?) 1 in 5 Americans claimed to be overloaded with information. Mind you, that was in the innocent halcyon days of 2016.

The acronym itself has also now mutated and diversified so that often the exclamation 'TMI!' means that too much intimate information has been divulged and can also cover the feeling one gets when seeing what there is to watch on Netflix.

(TMI is also a 1993 track by Duran Duran and an audio walk around Manchester.)

But TMI can have other disconcerting side-effects, from car drivers to people with autism.

B) WHY THEY SAID IT

In the UK around 1 in 100 people are on the autism spectrum. One element of autism that is neglected by the public is that being autistic means 'seeing, hearing and feeling the world in a different, often more intense way to other people'.

The UK's National Autism Society has been campaigning on a 'too much information' platform since 2016 to show the stress and anxiety that can be engendered when too much information is presented to people with autism.

They created their first film featuring 11-year-old Alex Marshall, which went viral, with over 56 million people viewing it on social media, and over one million also sharing it. The advert featured a child experiencing dramatic sensory overload in a shopping centre, making him feel overwhelmed and out of control. It ends with him plaintively stating, *"I'm not naughty, I'm autistic and I just get too much information."*

A second advert featured a schoolgirl drowning in the cacophony of everyday questioning and chatter, commenting *"It's as if my brain is too crowded – and about to explode."*

Companies are also trying to square one particular circle as consumers want them to be transparent – as honest and open as possible. But this then creates a potential TMI problem: so, the BBC has been forced to publish salaries of all its higher earning employees and employees of Zappos, the online shoe brand, were told they have 'a duty of transparency'. But this approach turns out to be divisive: many appreciate it, but others feel it is confusing and time-consuming. A London Business School analysis also cited an advertising agency chief complaining that too much transparency between client and agency can actually impair the creative process.

One final instance.

In February 2019, Essex County Council was in the news for losing an appeal against a driver's fine for going through a narrow bus gate. The council had previously earned £1.5 million from 54,000 drivers fined using the Chelmsford bus gate in the previous 18 months. But with the power of academic psychology behind her, Bernardine King had her fine quashed.

The gate, she argued forcibly, was filled with so many contradictory signs and messages that the average brain could not process all the information in such a short space of time and was simply unable to make the optimal decision (at least in the eyes of Essex County Council's traffic department).

"Drivers are being trapped in the area and they're panicking," she said. "There are so many signs by the bus gate but a little contradiction in the brain means we cannot absorb all the information."

C) WHEN YOU SHOULD USE IT

- One of the main insights from the world of behavioural economics – for example, found in Daniel Kahneman's *Thinking, Fast and Slow* – is the principle of cognitive load. Making decisions (especially in stressful situations – aka always) imposes a cognitive burden on the brain, which means it is energy-consuming, depletes willpower and focus and therefore creates anxiety

- So, we need to break the long-standing link between more information and better decisions, more information and more happiness and clarity

- Be it road signs or how we communicate with people with autism, we need to rethink information and how we transmit and receive it

TAGS: acronym, behaviour change, information

31. "CONTINUOUS PARTIAL ATTENTION"

WHO SAID IT AND IN WHAT CONTEXT

There is no shortage of terms, coinages and acronyms to describe our response to the internet. For example, 'wilfing' was prevalent several years back, standing for 'what was I looking for' and referring to the habit/pastime of/obsession with aimlessly surfing the net.

'Continuous Partial Attention' (CPA) is a term that was coined by former Microsoft executive Linda Stone at the end of the 1990s to describe the increasingly dispersed nature of attention, especially in online environments at a time when commentators were beginning to talk of 'the Age of Interruption'.

Sci-fi writer and web theorist Cory Doctorow called the internet 'an eco-system of interruption technologies'. Now it is taken for granted that we are nearly all (and nearly always) wrapped in an unrelenting flow of interactions to which we can only grant our partial concentration.

Distraction isn't entirely new though. In *Burnt Norton*, T. S. Eliot wrote that we moderns were "distracted from distraction by distraction". In *Humboldt's Gift*, American author Saul Bellow made this comment:

"Society claims more and more of your inner self and infects you with its restlessness. It trains you in distraction, colonizes consciousness as fast as consciousness advances."

And in an afterword to his *Collected Stories*, Bellow developed this theme, making no attempt to disguise his feelings about this disorder:

"Others have acquired a taste for distraction, and they freely consent to be addled. It may even seem to many that by being agitated they are satisfying the claims of society. The scope of the disorder can even be oddly flattering: Just look – this tremendous noisy frantic monstrous agglomeration ... And we are it! This is us!"

B) WHY THEY SAID IT

The issue of attention deficit culture and cognitive dexterity has become a battleground.

Steven Johnson's *Everything Bad Is Good for You* argues that despite the superficial comments, this more intense, fragmented exposure to media (including gaming) is enhancing our cognitive skills and non-literary popular culture is honing different mental capacities. On the other side of this neuro-wall is *The Shallows: what the internet is doing to our brains* by Nicholas Carr. The neuroscientist Baroness Susan Greenfield sides with the 'internet is changing our brains and not in a good way' side.

Linda Stone also distinguished between CPA and multitasking. Whereas multitasking was driven by an active goal for productivity and efficiency, CPA in her eyes was an automatic process, motivated only by a desire to connect and stay connected, in an effort to not miss anything that is going on. We may even say this was an early indication of FOMO (fear of missing out).

Compared to multitasking, full attention is not required by CPA (hence the 'partial') and the process is ongoing rather than episodic (hence the 'continuous'). Ultimately, CPA is motivated not by productivity but by connectivity.

c) WHEN YOU SHOULD USE IT

- The brain tends toward the cognitively miserly because it is so energy hungry and therefore energy-efficient; it tends toward what is simple and effortless. System 1, in Kahneman's terminology, is easily seduced and distracted and the more effortful and focused System 2 often needs to come to the party and tell System 1 to focus

- Therefore, we may need to pause to reflect, focus and re-focus, and consciously think a problem through before taking steady steps forward in an intentional direction

TAGS: acronyms, brain, behaviour

32. "THE DATA DUVET"

WHO SAID IT AND IN WHAT CONTEXT

The 'Data Duvet' is a term coined to describe the feeling of carefree cosiness that many presenters, commentators, analysts and politicians feel when they are snugly ensconced in a comforting blanket of data: as if the data confers a sense of warmth and complacency which means that the mere display of facts (especially numbers) is enough in itself to earn some reward.

The data might be a compendious array of statistics and facts, or simply the desire to fill all available white space so that they create the impression of being comprehensive (though comprehensively dull might be the output).

Just because the likes of Pythagoras (c 570-495 BCE) argued that 'numbers are gods' should not be enough of a reason to be oblivious to the fact that our brains are not designed to run Excel and we need human emotions to supplement any numbers or facts we are faced with.

There is no official TOG equivalent – the unit of warmth created at the Shirley Institute in Manchester and probably originating from the word 'togs' meaning clothing which, in turn, might come from the Roman toga; but the warmth of the duvet will often depend on the insecurity of the person sheltering beneath it.

B) WHY THEY SAID IT

The data duvet should be a warning to all those who feel that if we have enough data, statistics, facts or even infographics, we can avoid sticking our head above the parapet of perspective.

It is simply not enough for businesses to waste time being presented with 'death by PowerPoint' decks which are all content and no insight. We need to recognize the data duvet for what it is: a comforting wrapping of smug ostrich-style negligence at a time when a direction, a hypothesis, a point of view and guidance are what is being sought above all else.

Purveyors of research and analysts can be (but not exclusively) the worst offenders, since data is their realm. But there is an ingrained tendency to mistake means for ends: data is merely the oil in the engine, but it must be put to use in the pursuit of insight, innovation and novelty.

That means we must have the confidence (so often the real challenge) not to let data obscure the real point of a presentation: that of persuasion and advice.

C) WHEN YOU SHOULD USE IT

- Think of the data duvet as an aide-memoire when you or colleagues or suppliers are presenting data and you feel you are not really being provoked, guided or challenged

- Ask yourself:
  a) 'Am I deliberately being given a plethora of data because this person/company is trying to obscure the fact that they have nothing to say?!'
  b) 'Am I aware that I should have the courage myself to present a point of view, an angle or a direction from my data; and that I should expect that from anyone doing the same?'

TAGS: information, persuasion, neologism

33. VINYL HANDICAPPING CARTOON

A) WHO SAID IT AND IN WHAT CONTEXT

A *New Yorker* cartoon from May 2015 by Alex Gregory shows two men, one showing the other his extensive collection of turntables and speakers, saying:

> *"The two things that really drew me to vinyl were the expense and the inconvenience."*

At one level this is a reminder of the unexpected resurgence of vinyl after its near-extinction in the early 2000s. After bottoming out at less than 1 million copies in 2005, sales of new vinyl albums rose to 9.2 million copies in 2018, as reported by Nielsen Music. According to some analysts, vinyl sales may have been even larger as many industry data sources in the US do not include used vinyl. The Verge network recorded analysis indicating sales grew by just shy of 12% from 8.6 to 9.7 million sales. Not up there with streaming, but not what had been predicted in the digital era.

The 'vinyl revival' has also been aided by the annual Record Store Day, inaugurated in 2008 and designed to celebrate independent record stores. Vinyl features heavily, with bands such as Arcade Fire often releasing limited-edition vinyl tracks.

B) WHY THEY SAID IT

As with most cartoons, they operate at different levels: the wit, humour and insight showing us a disparity between what is said and what is intended. In this case, bringing attention to the unanticipated growth of vinyl (especially among the hipsters in his cartoon).

But perhaps without knowing, he is also acknowledging a psychological insight that has been behind a new understanding of elements of human behaviour across the range of brand consumption, communication and beyond, namely 'costly signalling'.

At a rational level, cost and inconvenience should be barriers to choice, rather than motivations to purchase.

The origins of the theory were in behavioural ecology and anthropology where experts garnered much evidence in favour of animal signalling. It hit the mainstream when, in the 1970s, Israeli biologist Amotz Zahavi argued in *The Handicap Principle* that these costs are an adaptive feature rather than a maladaptive fault. He proposed that sexually-selected traits have to be costly in order that they can act as precisely reliable indicators of an animal's fitness as a potential mate and parent.

Zahavi called these costly displays 'handicaps', because their ability to indicate fitness in the *reproductive* domain acted in a way that would directly reduce fitness in the survival domain.

C) WHEN YOU SHOULD USE IT

- The Handicap Principle explains much of human (consumer) behaviour and why luxury items often appear to be the most pointless and wasteful ones. They are evidence of costly authentication. If I can afford such outrageous fripperies, I must be a good genetic bet

- It also explains – for those of us in media, branding and communications – why the mere presence on TV suggests a brand is good. In Zahavi's terms, it indicates reliability and worth and the actual content of that signal is less important than is commonly thought

TAGS: behaviour, brands, communication

34. "ISN'T SHE RATHER SMALL AND FLAT?"

A) WHO SAID IT AND IN WHAT CONTEXT

Yes, it's a Picasso.

In his majestic sweep of the terrain of consciousness, the Danish science writer Tor Nørretranders wrote eloquently in *The User Illusion* of how little our *conscious* brain knows or does in our lives. As part of his thesis, he argues that our conscious brain is mostly given a simulation of the world, and that has profound implications for phenomena such as optical illusions, humour, sleeping, perception, learning and much more. We don't merely (or actually) see, we simulate. Nørretranders feels we need to be more aware of this gap, which he calls the 'user illusion'.

In his book, Nørretranders cites a variety of scientists, for instance John Gregory, the British neuropsychologist:

"The senses do not give us a picture of the world directly; rather they provide evidence for the checking of hypotheses about what lies before us."

But the quote from *The User Illusion* that brings us here is an anecdote about Picasso, first cited in Heinz R. Pagels' *The Dreams of Reason* (1988).

Picasso was once approached on a train by a stranger who asked why he didn't paint people "the way they really are". Picasso asked the man what he meant, so he pulled out a picture of his wife from his wallet, and said, "that's my wife".

"Isn't she rather small and flat?" responded Picasso.

B) WHY THEY SAID IT

Our world is a hypothesis, an interpretation. We see the map not the territory, in the words of Polish-American scientist and philosopher Alfred Korzybski.

This is rather like the Necker cube, the optical illusion, (technically an 'ambiguous figure'), created in 1832 by Swiss crystallographer and geographer, Louis Albert Necker, where we can see two alternative representations of a cube and one can flip to the other. This reminds us of the importance of perception in generating our reality.

"We do not see what we sense," says Nørretranders, "we see what we think we sense and what we experience has already acquired meaning before we are aware of it."

The Picasso anecdote reminds us that the picture is not more 'real' or 'true' than his Cubist representations. It is simply a convention of Western art that we have become accustomed to.

This story is accompanied by an anthropological tale of perspective, involving a tribe who were only ever used to judging animals from within the forest that the tribe inhabited. One day the anthropologist Colin Turnbull took the tribal guide to observe some buffalo some miles away in the distance. The guide asked what sort of insects they were. They drove closer to the buffalo, which obviously increased in size, but to the tribal guide this was only witchcraft. (See also Number 62, Small, Far Away ...')

C) WHEN YOU SHOULD USE IT

• Another reminder about the need to examine assumptions and not take the given for granted. What we think we see is being mediated by our brain, meaning that expectations and beliefs dictate a lot of what we actually see

• Art and science constantly tell us of the importance of perception and how much of our reality is a construction of the brain, most of which is an accurate representation of the territory, but sometimes the map will deceive us

TAGS: perceptions, behaviour, myths, storytelling

35. PHYSICS ENVY

The modern era has witnessed the ascendancy of science. In the realm of science, we have seen the shift from the primacy of physics to the supremacy of biology. How this happened can be amply demonstrated by the quote from the eminent physicist, Steve Weinberg, author of the cosmological treatise *The First Three Minutes:*

"You've seen one electron, you've seen em all."

Developmental biologist Lewis Wolpert, in *The Unnatural Nature of Science*, is equally forthright:

"In a sense all science aspires to be like physics, and physics aspires to be like mathematics."

This was more brutally expressed by no less an authority than James Watson, Nobel laureate and celebrated co-discoverer of the structure of DNA, as quoted in Steven Rose's book *Lifelines*.

> *"There is only one science – physics: everything else is social work."*

B) WHY THEY SAID IT

Biology is plainly not physics and an increasingly populous and vocal army of practitioners and writers in the sciences have come out and undermined the old order.

An even more elegant way of putting this fact is from Steven Rose, in *Alas, Poor Darwin*, a collection of essays devoted to attacking the ultra-Darwinians.

"In biology 1+1= 59."

One of the great enemies of the 'Physics is All' camp was philosopher, former Classicist and contrarian Mary Midgley. Much of her philosophical venom (for example, in *Science as Salvation*) was directed at those who think that physics (or indeed science at its broadest) can save the world.

Her prime target was the search for a single and fundamental level of reality and the belief that reductionist science (rather than the humanities) was the ultimate way of finding these truths. She saw scientists as dangerously prone to this tendency, and she castigated in particular those who saw physics as that fundamental answer.

Even more vitriol was dispensed by Steven Rose, who argued that reductive biology "is a science built on violence, on murdering to dissect". He was in favour of replacing the concept of a hierarchy with what he termed 'epistemological pluralism'.

c) WHEN YOU SHOULD USE IT

- What lies at the heart of the decline in many areas of business such as marketing is a reliance on the sanctity of science and, in particular, physics

- Too often we are prone to physics envy, a seductively alluring reductionist scheme that offers the promise of certainty. In advertising and research, the single criterion used to be 'Day After Recall', asking how many people remembered seeing an advert the morning after it aired; then the Awareness Index was devised by Gordon Brown in 1986, a black box metric, alleging a relationship between TV ratings and advertising recall. More recently it's the Net Promoter Score or the promise of using Influencers in social media – one metric, one model to save them all. What I like to think of as 'the Lure of the Single Criterion' is an unhelpful and pernicious wild goose chase in order to give us false hope of escaping the nightmare of imprecision

- In business, the physics-based approach has ensured the continued use of wobbly reassurances such as quantitative research in the hope of creating a sense of brand safety and predictability

TAGS: behaviour, advertising, science

36. "WHICH COMES FIRST – THE WORDS OR THE MUSIC?"

A) WHO SAID IT AND IN WHAT CONTEXT

A theme of all great philosophers, in or out of public houses, is the 'which came first' debate. Often it is 'the chicken or egg'. But another version concerns those of a musical bent: which comes first, the words or the music?

American Lyricist Sammy Cahn had an answer. In his *Songwriter's Rhyming Dictionary*, he states:

> *"I am often asked, which comes first – the words or the music? I answer that what comes first is the phone call asking you to write a song."*
>
> *"I don't need to be inspired," he added, "I just have to be hired."*

Sammy Cahn, (1913-1993), belonged to the golden age of American musicals and was one of the 20th century's most successful and acclaimed lyricists. Alongside Saul Chaplin, Jule Styne and later, through Frank Sinatra-Jimmy Van Heusen, he wrote the words for dozens of standards such as *High Hopes*, *My Kind of Town (Chicago is)*, *Let It Snow* and *Three Coins in the Fountain*.

Here it was, just like in the movies, a Jewish kid from the Lower East Side who, in five minutes, could turn corny clichés into No. 1 hits.

According to a *New York Times* review, he was born with a golden typewriter in his mouth: although as was typical of the age, a NYT review of his April 1974 show 'Words and Music' seems harshly acerbic to us now:

> *"Mr Cahn is not a great lyricist, as such, like Cole Porter or Stephen Sondheim, but he has a rare profes-sionalism that inspires music ... a subject matter that ranges from the ordinary to the ordinary, a touch of genius and a touch of love, and that is what makes Sammy run ... Mr Cahn's piano playing is worse than his singing, and that is the kindest thing one can say about it."*

Some were more flattering:

> *"The award-winner, 'Call Me Irresponsible' (1963), was among his best lyrics: to pack a love-song with five-syllable words and make them sound entirely nat-ural is a notable achievement – especially (as he liked to add) for a guy from a one-syllable neighbourhood."*

B) WHY THEY SAID IT

Cahn was not the first to offer his opinion on this vexed topic.

German composer Richard Strauss wrote an entire opera on the subject, *Capriccio*, in which a composer and a poet-librettist debate relentlessly whether it is 'prima la musica, poi le parole'. Based on an idea by Austrian novelist Stefan Zweig – and further back from Antonio Salieri – the action takes place at a gathering to celebrate the birthday of Countess Madeleine. A poet, Olivier, and composer Flamand provide the scene for a passionate discussion on what is more important, words or music, as they each seek to win the affection of the Countess.

And – spoiler alert – she declares a tie, concluding that both men interested her equally, the verdict Strauss himself was advocating.

C) WHEN YOU SHOULD USE IT

- Cahn was always perceived as an economical lyricist:
  - a) *'Give me Five Minutes More/Only Five Minutes More/ Let me stay/Let me stay in your arms.'*
  - b) *"What's wrong?" asked his composer, Jule Styne. "You got a stammer?" In its day, 'Five Minutes More' outsold the entire Gershwin catalogue. "What about these days," I asked. "Ah," replied Sammy. "That's the difference between a hit and a standard."*

- We can learn from Sammy Cahn that words do not always have to be the mysterious output of a muse. Any creative person will tell you that two of the most important springboards for creativity are constraints to work within – without them you have anarchy – and a deadline – which fosters imagination

37. "THE OPPOSITE OF PLAY ISN'T WORK, IT'S DEPRESSION"

WHO SAID IT AND IN WHAT CONTEXT

This was cited in Pat Kane's *The Play Ethic*, and attributed to Brian Sutton-Smith, the former dean of Play Studies at the University of Pennsylvania. Born in New Zealand, but working in the US till his death in 2015, Sutton-Smith was a pioneer in play, working across many disciplines from education and psychology to folklore. In books such as *The Ambiguity of Play* he argued that there were many forms or 'rhetorics' of play, which should encompass child's play all the way to sport, gambling, festivals, imagination and nonsense.

The High Priest of *The Play Ethic* is former musician Pat Kane – half of the 80s Scottish rock band Hue and Cry. Kane gave a detailed and constructive critique of the drawbacks of the current work ethic, and outlined a manifesto for how play needs to be integrated into all parts of our life.

Kane's hypothesis is that to fully embrace the 'play ethic' and reject the work ethic means that a 'player' must be 'wilful, exultant and committed' and in so doing we can widen our conception of who we are and what we might be capable of.

B) WHY THEY SAID IT

In this argument, Kane takes aim against what he sees as 'arid social rationalism', the draining of fun and play from the world of work and leisure. For Kane, play is a generator of originality and energy, and we are enjoined to 'create and act, more than just spectate and consume.' For this we need, space, time and materials to play.

The creative side of play is something espoused (unsurprisingly) by Will Wright, game designer and creator of 'The Sims'. Wright co-founded Electronic Arts and in 2007 was the first game designer to be awarded a fellowship by BAFTA, The British Academy of Film and Theatre Arts.

"We're always building models of the world around us to help predict what's going to happen, and play is one of the primary ways in which we build these models. I think storytelling lives alongside play as another mechanism for building models," Will Wright quoted in *The Art of Immersion*, by Frank Rose.

Or take the ethos of the Danish toy brand Lego, which has been based from the beginning on an appreciation of the link between play and education. Originally derived from the Danish for 'play well', it is also said to have been chosen because of its links with the Latin word 'lego', meaning 'I read'. The company has always insisted on the umbilical link between play and learning in what it calls 'creative construction'.

Actors see this in their jobs. Here is Daniel Day-Lewis in an interview with *The Guardian*'s Simon Hattenstone:

> *"The important thing is it's a game. And that's what people misunderstand. It's a game, a very elaborate one. But as far as possible each of us is trying to go back to the playpen to retrieve that state of naïvety … so it's a game and a game is a pleasurable thing. The work is pleasure, yet it is always presented as a form of elaborate self-flagellation."*

C) WHEN YOU SHOULD USE IT

- Gamification has become something of a buzzword in business for taking the essence of games – fun, play, transparency, design and challenge – and applying it to beyond mere entertainment so as to 'engage the consumer': for example, in gathering market research responses or encouraging people to visit or stay on websites

- But as Kane and co suggest, playfulness needs re-evaluation. It must be placed at the centre of our lives if we want to maintain (or develop) a sense of creativity, wellbeing and what psychologists term 'effectance': the belief that we can make a difference and have an impact

TAGS: creativity, play, psychology

38. "ULTRACREPIDARIANISM"

A) WHO SAID IT AND IN WHAT CONTEXT

Mark Forsyth is a writer, etymologist and another alumnus of Lincoln College, Oxford. He has written many books and articles on the topic of etymology, after starting his 'Inky Fool' blog in 2009. His book, *The Etymologicon*, a witty, erudite and thematically linked analysis of etymological origins, proved a surprise Christmas bestseller in 2011 in the line of *Schott's Miscellany* and Lynne Truss's *Eats, Shoots and Leaves* (see Number 25).

He followed this in 2012 with *The Horologicon*, another ramble through the byways and paths of the English language, loosely named after the hours of the day. In this he said:

> *"It is for the words too beautiful to live long, too amusing to be taken seriously, too precise to become common, too vulgar to survive polite society, or too poetic to thrive in the age of prose."*

One of the entries is 'ultracrepidarian', a word that both has a deep and convoluted history, but also finds itself with a renewed vitality in this age of internet bubbles of outrage.

B) WHY THEY SAID IT

The origin of this delightful word goes back to one Apelles of Cos, a renowned 4th century BCE painter. None of his work survives but our main source is Roman author and naturalist Pliny the Elder (1st century CE), among whose works was the encyclopaedic – 37 books' worth – *Historia Naturalis*. Apelles was said to have made painted portraits of Alexander the Great, perhaps even the one of which a copy survives at the Villa of the Faun in Pompeii.

Pliny tells what must have been, by his time, a legendary story of Apelles's habit of leaving his paintings out for public display and hiding behind them to overhear the public's responses. One day, a cobbler examined one of his works and commented that there was an error with the sandal. Apelles duly corrected this overnight, only for the cobbler to return in the morning and criticize the subject's leg. To which Apelles then allegedly retorted:

"Ne sutor ultra crepidam (iudicaret)."

Literally, 'let the cobbler not judge beyond the sole'. In other words, he may know about shoes, but beyond that he should keep other artistic judgments to himself.

This is probably behind the English proverb: '*A cobbler should stick to his last*'.

The English essayist and painter William Hazlitt is generally considered to have coined the term 'ultracrepidarian' in English for a specific purpose, to denigrate poet and critic William Gifford, editor of *The Quarterly Review*, in a letter in 1819, described as 'one of the finest works of invective in the language'.

"You have been well called an Ultra-Crepidarian critic."

There is another reason why for Gifford this shoe fitted so well: before attending Exeter College, Oxford, Gifford had served an apprenticeship ... to a shoemaker.

C) WHEN YOU SHOULD USE IT

- As rebukes go, ultracrepidarian may lack some of the spittling, visceral ferocity of other options, but there is something very topical about it. At this time, when experts are vilified many are fearful of leaving their chosen area of expertise – consider someone like Richard Dawkins and how he has been regularly vilified for his trenchant views on religion

- And working in the advertising business, one is often confronted with people who because they see adverts on TV, posters, in their feeds feel that that is enough to make them experts, without having any theory of how adverts (or people) work

- On a lighter note, an insult that will always go down well in these Twitter-storm-tossed times is 'you don't know what you're talking about'. The typical football crowd, used to chanting at the referee (or a rival manager, or even in extremis, their own labouring manager) are wont to cry 'you don't know what you're doing'

- I personally long to go to Old Trafford, visit the Kop, the Emirates or the Etihad and witness a crowd of football fans chant 'the ref's ultracrepidarian', a wish that might be long in the making

39. PARTY CANNON

A) WHO SAID IT AND IN WHAT CONTEXT

Not so much as what they said but how. The case of the Party Cannon Death Metal sore thumb.

If you want to look at genre convention, tribal loyalties and fierce visual protectionism, the semiotics of Death Metal are not a bad place to start.

For their poster promoting their appearance at the Bay Area Deathfest II in California in July 2015, the band chose to subvert the semiotics of the genre. Rather than the spikey, spindly Gothic lettering, theirs was Candy Crush – gleeful and ostentatiously childlike. This made them stand out against the other bands performing, such as Cattle Decapitation, Psycroptic or Devourment. And Brian Blessed (the band not the bloke).

Party Cannon originate from Dunfermline, Scotland and are currently signed with Gore House Productions: their releases include 2015's 'Bong Hit Hospitalisation' and the 2013 live album 'Drunk in Cambridge'.

They are described on Encyclopaedia Metallum (it's as if none of these guys every studied Latin) as belonging to the genre of 'brutal Death Metal' (is there a scale?) with lyrical themes covering 'corporate control, war operation, decay of Earth, humour and (last but not least) partying'.

But their cutesy Toys 'R' Us logo even made it onto Wired and Buzzfeed.

B) WHY THEY SAID IT

The band acknowledged that the poster had gone viral several times already.

"People in the brutal Death Metal community don't prescribe to the elitism some other genres do, which makes it all the better. Plus, they're kinda playing in to our hands by getting pissy about the logo; that's the point."

But whether they were marketing geniuses (not the toughest job in Death Metal, arguably), they have unknowingly been cited by marketing and communications commentators for their avoidance of convention and self-parody and attention to the needs of brand differentiation.

Though described as 'punishingly heavy', their atypical typography has certainly carved out their own niche.

C) WHEN YOU SHOULD USE IT

- Pretty much every time the poster is rediscovered, social media overflows with adoration for the brand, the consensus being in the words of Wired that 'it is genius'. Other adulation takes the form of 'my new favourite Death Metal band', 'let's play spot the biggest badass' and more candidly, 'Party Cannon f*cking rules'

- More than this, they took a stand against the convention of flamboyant undecipherability, which may be part of what makes the semiotics right for that tribe. So even in a tightly-knit herd like Death Metal, it pays to be eye-catching by avoiding cliché, going against the grain and bucking the trend

- In branding and advertising terms, the need for saliency has long been recognized as the *sine qua non* of communications. If you aren't being noticed, is your money (time/energy) being wasted?

- So, we have the unlikely occurrence of the mainstream communications world learning a lesson many shouldn't need to from a Death Metal party slam band. Examining assumptions, conventions and clichés and then subverting them can work in so many ways to create differentiation and memorability

TAGS: advertising, brands, saliency

40. "THERE ARE TWO KINDS OF PEOPLE IN THE WORLD ..."

"There are two kinds of people in the world: those who divide people into two classes and those who don't."

A) WHO SAID IT AND IN WHAT CONTEXT

This caught the eye in December 2013 when it was tweeted by astronomer Neil deGrasse Tyson, but goes back to American writer Robert Benchley. However, I want to explore its use in Steven Pinker's *How the Mind Works* (we saw Pinker in Number 13).

This was Pinker's early investigation of the machinery of mind: the origins, development and nature of the mind, based on his research from the domain of evolutionary psychology and beyond. Pinker first argues – not to everyone's taste – that the mind is purely a product of ultra-Darwinian principles, ensuring it is driven by pressures to enhance survival and reproductive success; and secondly that it is inherently modular.

As part of his dissection of the brain, he explores the brain's tendency to categorize, and this is where he quotes Robert Benchley (see below). Pinker's main answer is that placing items into categories allows us to infer and predict.

The full quote continues in the same vein:

"There are two kinds of people in the world: those who divide people into two classes and those who don't. Both classes are extremely unpleasant to meet socially, leaving practically no one in the world whom one cares very much to know."

B) WHY THEY SAID IT

Robert Benchley (1889-1945) was an American actor and critic. He became managing editor of *Vanity Fair*, worked with Dorothy Parker and became a leading light of the Algonquin Round Table, a cabal of comics, writers and wits, informally – and quite smugly – referred to as the 'Vicious Circle'.

But though prolific on radio and in film, his greatest renown accrued from his essays. Benchley's aphorism appeared in a literary review of *The New York City Telephone Directory*. Benchley's review criticized its 'plot', declaring, "It lacks coherence. It lacks stability."

Other evidence of Benchley's wit includes:

"The free-lance writer is a man who is paid per piece or per word or perhaps."

"Drawing on my fine command of the English language, I said nothing."

Often his wit was related anecdotally. According to the actor David Niven's memoir, *The Moon's a Balloon*, on a summer vacation trip Benchley arrived in Venice and immediately wired him:

'STREETS FLOODED. PLEASE ADVISE.'

c) WHEN YOU SHOULD USE IT

• As they say, a great idea (or joke) has many parents; a bad idea (or joke) is an orphan. Benchley's original has been wrongly ascribed to many others and has certainly diversified and flourished

• One version was printed in the *Journal of Research and Development in Education*: *"I once heard that there are two kinds of people: those who couch everything in dichotomies and those who do not."*

• Slightly better known (especially in mathematical circles) is: *"There are only 10 kinds of people in the world: those who understand binary, and those who don't."*

- Yet, this is not merely a clever observation, but a critique of those who are obsessed with over-classification. In the business world – especially in marketing and research – the tendency to turn concepts into things, to atomize, classify and reduce, is widespread and can tend to the arid reductionism which we have criticized elsewhere

41. "ANYONE CAN DO ANY AMOUNT OF WORK PROVIDED ..."

"Anyone can do any amount of work provided that it is not the work he is supposed to be doing at that moment."

A) WHO SAID IT AND IN WHAT CONTEXT

In their book, *Willpower: Rediscovering the Greatest Human Strength*, psychologist Roy F. Baumeister and *New York Times* journalist John Tierney praised the virtue of self-control, insisting that it can be nurtured, and detailed Baumeister's seminal research. Baumeister is best known for having built on Walter Mischel's marshmallow experiments on delayed gratification.

Baumeister argues that willpower is like a muscle: it can be exercised, trained and can even lead to greater happiness. But, famously, Baumeister coined the term 'ego depletion' to express the idea that willpower is rationed, and we make bad decisions when tired or stressed. Part of his argument is that the exercising of self-control depletes our glucose, which makes us more likely to succumb to later temptations.

Equally, replenishing our stock of glucose restores our ego.

In the course of a discussion about procrastination, Tierney and Baumeister mention members of the Algonquin Round Table and their aversion to deadlines (Dorothy Parker once blamed the delay on a piece on the fact that 'somebody was using the pencil').

At the heart of Baumeister's work was a study from 1996 by Baumeister and his wife Dianne Tice using chocolate cookies and radishes, and a lab smelling of fresh cookies. One group of student guinea pigs were left with cookies to eat, the other were left with radishes: then both were given a fiendish puzzle – actually insoluble – to work on after.

Those who ate the radishes made far fewer attempts and devoted less than half the time (eight minutes) to solving the puzzle compared to the chocolate cookie-eating participants (19 minutes) and a control group: ipso facto, self-control could be regulated. The results showed that turning down the allure of confectionery affected their will and ability to engage in a demanding task.

The study had a huge impact and created a vast legacy besides, although it has fallen prey to the 'reproducibility' crisis that is affecting much of social psychology, where seminal experiments seem to be unable to be repeated, thus demonstrating their validity.

B) WHY THEY SAID IT

Benchley, in a typically wry column, 'How to Get Things Done: One Week in the Life of a Writing Man', published in the *Chicago Tribune* on 2 February 1930, outlined his psychological principle of what might be called 'studied task avoidance'.

A master of procrastination, he elaborated with typical wit on his philosophy of positive self-deception: he would compile a list with what was meant to be the most important task to be accomplished at the top, but instead moved it to the bottom.

This might mean sharpening pencils, making plans, composing a reply to a friend's letter that had been sitting for years on a pile on his desk, changing typewriter ribbons, relighting his pipe, building a book shelf and clipping pictures of tropical fish out of magazines – Benchley did get down to work and would accomplish many worthwhile activities, but not necessarily the most important one.

c) WHEN YOU SHOULD USE IT

- Benchley's thinking was echoed and developed in John Perry's *Structured Procrastination* and *Don't Buy This Book Now!*, just one of many books, columns and scattered outpourings on the vexed topic of productivity

- This seems to many an important psychological insight that is worth quoting and indeed pursuing: working with the brain's idiosyncrasies rather than against them

TAGS: humour, productivity, behavioural economics

"42"

WHO SAID IT AND IN WHAT CONTEXT

In the same way that it might be the dead parrot, the knights who go 'ni' and silly walks for fans of Monty Python, a tribe of fans and followers greet, acknowledge and amuse each other by referring to Marvin the Paranoid Android, the Babel fish, Vogon poetry, Zaphod Beeblebrox and the Improbability Drive.

Douglas Adams wrote *The Hitchhiker's Guide to the Galaxy* initially as a BBC radio series in 1978 before it colonized other media: first a trilogy of five books, then a TV series, a play, computer game and then, after his sadly premature death at the age of 49 in 2001, a mediocre film.

Bands such as Level 42 and Radiohead (in their 1997 'OK Computer' album, and the track 'Paranoid Android') all paid homage to Adams and *The Hitchhiker's Guide*.

B) WHY THEY SAID IT

In H2G2 (its normal abbreviation), 42 is the answer to the ultimate question of Life, the Universe and Everything.

It was eventually computed and revealed by the supercomputer Deep Thought after taking a while to think it over (seven and a half million years to be precise). The answer then led to the construction of a next generation computer, whose task was to work out the question in the first place. That computer was named (spoiler alert) Earth.

The Hitchhiker's series begins with the imminent destruction of the Earth by Vogons to make way for a hyperspace bypass, five minutes before Earth was destined to deliver its answer. So, although the Earth was often mistakenly considered as a planet, it was in fact a powerful supercomputer running a programme designed by a race of hyper-intelligent, pan-dimensional beings known to us as mice. And according to *The Hitchhiker's Guide to the Galaxy*, the Earth is 'mostly harmless'.

Deep Thought did warn those sent to hear its oracular response that they wouldn't like it.

The legacy of 42 lives on: the house number of the UK sitcom *The Kumars at No 42* was selected because one of the writers, Sanjeev Bhaskar, was a huge H2G2 fan; the IBM chess-playing supercomputer was named Deep Thought in honour of the series; the US TV series *Lost* had a series of mysterious numbers (4, 8, 15, 16, 23), which intentionally ended with 42, and the number recurs throughout the series. Another celebrated use is 42 Wallaby Way – the address on the diving mask in Pixar's *Finding Nemo*. And a final example, the office of former Google CEO, Eric Schmidt, is called Building 42.

A book written in 2011 by dedicated fan and investigator Peter Gill, *42: Douglas Adams' Amazingly Accurate Answer to Life, the Universe and Everything* sought playfully to examine why 42 is indeed the answer.

C) WHEN YOU SHOULD USE IT

Adams was a marvellous combination of thinker, satirist and comic. The '42' idea and the reason for its memetic tenacity is both brilliant and simple. We are all looking for the answer, but much of the time is wasted because we haven't really understood or even identified the question.

Fans and geeks have tried to explain the significance, symbolic or otherwise, of the number 42. True, there have been instances of it, for example, in *Monty Python* and in Lewis Carroll's *Alice In Wonderland* (both clear influences). But despite Stephen Fry claiming Adams had revealed the secret to him, which he would take with him to his grave, the answer seems both more banal and realistic: it was a random number, Adams admitted, that just sounded funny.

In an interview on BBC radio's *Book Club* in 2000, Adams explained that: *"On my way to work one morning, still writing the scene and was thinking about what the answer should be. I decided it should be something that made no sense whatsoever – a number, and a mundane one at that."*

- So perhaps our conclusion in the case of 42 is that we should all seek to distance ourselves from the seemingly unquenchable thirst for 'An Answer To End All Answers'

- Elsewhere, in the marketing and business world, there is a compulsion to seek and measure one number that shows whether (for example) a piece of communication will work (these days measured in clicks or likes). But can we ever really reduce the complexity of human response to a single number, a single answer?

- Is 42 not actually a warning about what we might call 'runaway reductionism', the belief in some quarters that everything can be reduced to one number, one message, one rule or one diet?

TAGS: metrics, humour, behaviour

43. "NEED IS THE FALL GUY OF DESIRE"

A) WHO SAID IT AND IN WHAT CONTEXT

Adam Phillips is a psychoanalyst and writer, and generally considered to be 'Britain's foremost psychoanalytic writer', 'the superstar shrink', and one of the finest prose stylists in the language. He did, after all, read English at Oxford and is a Visiting Professor in the English department at the University of York.

A regular contributor to the *London Review of Books*, he has written some 20 works and is as much at home with literary criticism and etymology as in the pathways of the mind, believing that psychoanalysis is a series of stories that we tell ourselves and each other, a method of redescribing and understanding our experiences.

He writes using the virtuoso panoply of the rhetorician, aphoristically and epigrammatically: precious little of his writing does not benefit from (and sometimes demands) a reread to enjoy its depths. Even the droll titles: *On Kissing, Tickling and Being Bored:*

Psychoanalytic Essays on the Unexamined Life, *The Beast in the Nursery: On Curiosity and Other Appetites* and *Unforbidden Pleasures* reveal a love of language that is often dazzling and daunting, and occasionally dizzying.

Reading Phillips is never dull. Often a challenge, but never dull.

In *Darwin's Worms*, he writes:

> *"The person and the world ... are two turbulences enmeshed with each other."*

A loyal defender of Freudianism – or at least his own brand of it – Penguin books duly installed him as supervisor of the new English translation of Freud.

B) WHY THEY SAID IT

In *Side Effects*, his paean to a life replete with asides and tangents, Phillips explores French psychoanalyst Jacques Lacan. Psychoanalysis, argues Phillips, attends to 'side effects', so we should see where 'side effects' take us.

As so often with Phillips, it is easy to almost skid past something of note. It is here he says:

> *"In his view there is no such thing as pure need. All hungers are informed by, contaminated by, the pressure of desire ... need is the fall guy of desire."*

Arguably, this is one of Phillips's least dense aphorisms, but one that we can repurpose here to summarize much of the behavioural economics enterprise and beyond. As Phillips proposes, because we know so little about what we actually want, we are constantly justifying our unknown desires by rational needs.

In *Darwin's Worms*, Phillips looks at the cycle of death, destruction and rebirth by discussing Darwin's fascination with earthworms, and from there helping us understand death and loss.

Despite being instructed by his father, "You care for nothing but shooting, dogs, and rat-catching and you will be a disgrace to yourself and all your family," by most definitions Darwin turned out quite well. But as well as his revolutionary theory of natural selection, Darwin maintained a deep interest in earthworms over 40 years, including a 29-year experiment measuring the rate that a stone is buried by the burrowing activities of earthworms. Much of Darwin's book covers his work measuring the amount of earth brought to the surface by earthworms: he estimated that earthworms move 15 tons of soil per acre to the surface each year – a process now known as bioturbation. Darwin concluded that *"there are few animals which have played so important a part in the history of the world than the earthworm".*

Darwin published his findings in 1881 in *The Formation of Vegetable Mould through the Action of Worms, with Observations of their Habits*. The book sold 6,000 copies in its first year, selling faster than *On the Origin of Species* had when it was first published. It was his last work, published six months before he died.

c) WHEN YOU SHOULD USE IT

- So, any time when you feel that your needs, your rationality are in charge of your decisions or – if you work in business – in charge of your colleagues or consumers, recall these words and acknowledge that your needs are just a subterfuge for your desires

- These elegant aphorisms embody a deep-seated if uncomfortable truth that we have far less control over ourselves, our lives, our wants and our feelings than we would like to admit

- And never, ever underestimate a worm

TAGS: behaviour, desire

44. "WE DON'T SERVE TACHYONS HERE"

A) WHO SAID IT AND IN WHAT CONTEXT

Some backstory to the punchline. Except it isn't the punchline. And yet it is.

Nerd. Geek. Intellectual. All points on a spectrum of abuse directed by the militant wing of the humanities at scientists. Arts good, sciences bad: worse still, say the Artistes – the science guys have no sense of humour.

The Big Bang Theory (2007-2019) – featuring a group of physicists, aerospace engineers, an astrophysicist, neuroscientist and a microbiologist, and with cameos from the likes of Stephen Hawking – should have redressed the cultural balance to show that (albeit unwittingly) there is humour to be mined in science and scientists.

Some science jokes in time-honoured fashion (see Number 9) use the tribe or in-group as the butt of the humour to ensure factional loyalty. Take this jest submitted to *The Guardian* by mathematician, popularizer and Arsenal fan, Marcus du Sautoy, Professor for the Public Understanding of Science at Oxford University since 2008, a role he took over from Richard Dawkins.

> Q: How can you spot an extrovert mathematician?
> A: He looks at your shoes when he talks to you.

But let's return to the joke that brought us here. In full, it goes (and there are obvious varieties of telling):

> 'We don't serve tachyons here'. A tachyon walks into a bar.

B) WHY THEY SAID IT

To fully grasp the humour and simplicity of the joke, you need to have a rudimentary grasp of relativity theory and quantum physics. The tachyon is a hypothetical particle, which is supposed to travel faster than the speed of light: it was named by Gerald Feinberg of Columbia University from the word 'fast' in Greek as in tachometer.

The tachyon remains controversial, but many physicists believe that it is one of the many weird and untestable hypotheses – like the multiverse theory – which may yet be proved true.

The joke operates on the basis that the tachyon moves faster than the speed of light and so we get the punchline before the set-up.

In particular, particles do well in science jokes:

A neutron walks into a bar and asks: "'How much for a beer?" The bartender says, "For you? No charge."

And there are some other ace one-liners:

'If you're not part of the solution, you're part of the precipitate.'

Steve Jones, former head of the Department of Genetics at University College London, award-winning author of books such as *Almost Like a Whale: the Origin of Species Updated*, broadcaster and all-round Darwin fan offered this:

'Well, there was this homeopath who forgot to take his medicine and died of an overdose.'

A pithy, pointed and scathing attack on the principles (and popularity) of homeopathy: for any of those – and there are many in the scientific establishment – who feel homeopathy lacks evidence and should not receive any support within the UK's National Health Service, this one line does more than an elaborate, judgmental essay.

C) WHEN YOU SHOULD USE IT

- The Jones joke shows why we need jokes, insights and pithy observations. The essence of humour and wit is to encapsulate a truth in microcosm

- But jokes, as we have seen, also work as tribal glue, a lubricant for people to feel they are sharing values and worldviews; sometimes in a warm fashion to the exclusion of those who 'don't get it'

- And we could all do with building more bridges between the arts and the sciences

TAGS: humour, science, storytelling

45. NUMBER 45

A) WHO SAID IT AND IN WHAT CONTEXT

The story of a subversive teapot and a number that went viral in the 18th century.

In 2018, the British Museum hosted an exhibition called 'I Object', a collection of often scurrilous items that reflected the long British history of dissent.

Ian Hislop, the editor of the satirical magazine *Private Eye*, and BM curator Tom Hockenhull scoured the museum's artefacts and drawings to display a selection that reflects the British propensity for anger and opposition to authority.

It was a self-consciously eclectic exhibition, with everything from a deliciously fake cave painting by Banksy to a brick commissioned for a building by Nebuchadnezzar II in 500 BCE, who insisted on having his name inscribed on every brick but was also signed by the cheeky craftsman.

Let's focus instead on the 'jaunty piece of Worcester ware', aka a pretty teapot decorated in blue and picked out with gold with red flowers, dating from the 1760s.

But this was no mere hot beverage receptacle: this was an act of seditious protest and rebellion, with the number 45 subtly visible at the base of the spout.

B) WHY THEY SAID IT

Let's look into the history of this piece.

The number 45 was a symbol, a totem and a signal of rebellion in support of notorious political firebrand and radical Whig politician, John Wilkes.

Wilkes was a one-off: an MP, agitator, freedom fighter, hero to the American colonial rebels, demagogue, wit, pornographer, scandalous libertine and shameless self-promoter. His immorality was the stuff of legend, as was his behaviour at the Hellfire Club: when the Earl of Sandwich, a long-time friend, told him that "You will die either on the gallows, or of the pox." Wilkes replied, "That must depend on whether I embrace your lordship's principles or your mistress." Nice.

The specific dissent was in edition No 45 of the magazine *The North Briton*, published on 23 April 1763. It contained an incendiary attack on Lord Bute's ministry and, in particular, on King George III's speech to Parliament and with regard to the recent peace with France which Wilkes believed was too soft. Wilkes savaged the Tory parliamentary supporters of the despised King as the "the foul dregs of power, the tools of corruption and despotism". Despite, or perhaps because of, the populist tone, *The North Briton* sold 2,000 copies a week – nearly ten times the circulation of *The Briton*.

Unsurprisingly, King George III ordered Wilkes's arrest and ordered copies of *The North Briton* No 45 to be publicly burned, but the mob saved them from the bonfire. Of course, trying to burn something makes it more inflammatory (as it were), only adding to its seductive appeal. Wilkes was released a week later under 'Parliamentary Privilege' but went on to reprint the issue as well as other pamphlets. In breach of 'Privilege', he was expelled from Parliament and henceforth no longer protected by immunity.

Thereafter '45' was sported on brooches by his supporters, who chanted it at meetings and daubed it on hundreds of doors. During the 1760s, '45' became a shorthand for expressing radical and anti-monarchist sympathies. One might even call it a (fire) brand before its time.

c) WHEN YOU SHOULD USE IT

- The tale of the treasonable teapot can teach us much. Primarily, for anyone in the branding and communications world this is a familiarly prescient example of the power of the brand-as-shorthand: something that sums up a series of facts and information in a way that is simple to grasp and easily shared – viral, if you want to use that term

- It shows how something as easy to repeat and transmit as a number can be a form of secret code or language shared among a community, in this case a shared code among fans of Wilkes's subversive politics. As we have seen before, so much communication is about reinforcing a tribe or community through shared views

- If 45 can be a shorthand, how else can political or issue-based groups, or companies utilize something simple to promote their causes? What was 45 if not a brand/logo, and why don't we see more of it today?

TAGS: brand, communication, storytelling

46. "WHAT WE CALL RATIONAL GROUNDS FOR OUR BELIEFS ARE IRRATIONAL ATTEMPTS TO JUSTIFY OUR INSTINCTS"

A) WHO SAID IT AND IN WHAT CONTEXT

Thomas Henry Huxley (1825-1895) was an English biologist best known for his tenacious support of Darwin's theory of evolution, for which he gained the sobriquet 'Darwin's Bulldog'. He became an ardent public spokesman for the more reticent Darwin in the propagation of Darwin's controversial ideas.

After sailing to the Southern Hemisphere to explore marine invertebrates, Huxley enjoyed a meteoric rise in reputation; Marian Evans (aka novelist George Eliot), who wrote alongside Huxley for the rationalist *Westminster Review*, realized he was equally driven by a desire for provocation.

As Darwin was preparing to publish *On the Origin of Species by Means of Natural Selection*, he invited Huxley to his home, Down House, in Kent, and the pair became fast friends. Though Huxley had trouble accepting all aspects of Darwin's theory of evolution, he passionately believed in its explanation of a non-miraculous and non-religious origin of speciation.

Reading 'the Origin' for the first time, Huxley declared: "How extremely stupid not to have thought of that."

A defining moment in the debate around and acceptance of Darwin's theories was Huxley's debate with William Wilberforce, Bishop of Oxford, in 1860 at the annual meeting of the British Association for the Advancement of Science centring around a famous exchange on 'being descended from apes'.

Much of the detail remains shrouded in myth, but Wilberforce was an implacable enemy of evolutionary ideas and had been coached by Richard Owen, the great anatomist and palaeontologist who later helped to found London's Natural History Museum (of which he became the first superintendent). Owen is perhaps less well known these days than he should be for coining the word 'dinosaur' (meaning 'terrifying lizard', though the media occasionally likes to imply that he 'invented' dinosaurs).

Wilberforce apparently asked whether the apes were on Huxley's grandmother's or grandfather's line, which became probably the most famous soundbite of a memorably dramatic encounter. Its symbolic significance is now enshrined by a plaque at the Oxford University Museum of Natural History.

Wilberforce died tragically after being thrown by his horse. Sitting in the Athenaeum Club, Huxley wryly noted that the Bishop's brain had finally come into contact with reality and the result was fatal.

Huxley also famously coined the word 'agnosticism' in 1869 at a meeting of The Metaphysical Society as meaning *"... that a man shall not say he knows or believes that which he has no scientific grounds for professing to know or believe."*

B) WHY THEY SAID IT

But the quote which we began with was written as a note in *The Natural Inequality of Man* (1890), a critique of Jean-Jacques Rousseau's views of mankind's development.

It was cited in *Phantoms in the Brain* by V. S. Ramachandran, an Indian neuroscientist and Professor at University of California, San Diego, and listed in Time's 100 Most Influential People in The World in 2011.

The reason for its appearance in Ramachandran's work, and for its broader relevance, is that Huxley has encapsulated some truths that behavioural economists would happily rally around.

First, that we have perpetuated a myth that we are wholly creatures of rationality. Next, that decisions are predominantly the preserve of this rationality. And finally, that our base animal instincts are largely under our control.

C) WHEN YOU SHOULD USE IT

- Huxley's aphorism sums up the insight that we like to feel that many of our actions and attitudes are justified by rational facts and information-gathering when, in fact, (ugly truth), we are far more driven by our instincts (for which read emotions, evolutionary imperatives and the like) than we like to admit

- And even when we try to post-rationalize those instincts the rationality may be rather irrational

TAGS: science, behaviour

47. "A JUMBO JET IS COMPLICATED, BUT MAYONNAISE IS COMPLEX"

A) WHO SAID IT AND IN WHAT CONTEXT

Paul Cilliers was a South African philosopher, researcher and Professor in Complexity and Philosophy at the Stellenbosch University in South Africa's Western Cape Province. Cilliers is best known for his enduring contributions to the field of complex systems and complexity thinking.

This recent intellectual tradition, which Cilliers embodied and perpetuated, was in opposition to the dominant notion of reductionism in the science (see also Number 35, 'Physics Envy') of looking solely at isolating parts.

Instead, complexity and systems thinking sought to build bridges between the theories of post-structuralism or post-modernism (generally seen as hostile to science and scientists) and the emerging theory of emergence. This was the heart of his *Complexity and Postmodernism: Understanding Complex Systems*, which catapulted him into the heart of complexity thinking's superstars.

Complexity de-emphasizes the method of breaking things into chunks of 'stuff', instead building understanding based on a nest of holistic and interdependent processes. Pattern, flow and network are prioritized rather than essence and matter: traffic, bees, weather and human systems (sport, for example) all come under its purview.

One of the consequences is that small variations in the initial conditions can have huge effects on the end results, as exemplified in Edward Lorenz's famous 'butterfly effect' theory. Another is that the properties of a system are not necessarily inherent in the rules.

B) WHY THEY SAID IT

As part of Cilliers' promotion of complexity theory, he cites 'a French person' as the source of the metaphor (or simile) of jumbo jet vs. mayonnaise, and to that person we must say 'merci et félicitations'.

It is a wonderful analogy to explain a key tenet and principle at the heart of complexity thinking.

In brief, Cilliers' complexity theory implies that 'complicated' things can be explained satisfactorily by examining their component parts. 'Complex' ones cannot because they are greater than the sum of their parts.

Cilliers cites a metaphor of jumbo jet vs. mayonnaise, a wonderful analogy to explain a key tenet and principle at the heart of complexity thinking.

Replacing one part of a jumbo jet does not alter its fundamental structure or operation. With a complex object, such as mayonnaise, it is not merely more than the sum of its parts: if you change one ingredient, you change the whole mayonnaise (ask any cook). What matters – if not more than the ingredients – is the way they interact with each other to create the final outcome.

This observation holds true no matter how many parts are involved or even the cost of the object. And it means that whereas complicated products can be analysed, predicted and understood, this is not the case with those that are complex, where examination has to be holistic.

Nonlinear interactions produce emergent properties which cannot be predicted from the properties of the individual constituents. Biologist and complexity researcher Stuart Kauffman termed this 'order for free' (and he wasn't thinking of Amazon Prime).

C) WHEN YOU SHOULD USE IT

- If you are in the insight gathering business, one question to ask yourself is: are you sure you are not merely analysing your system in a reductionist sense, when you should be exploring it systematically and holistically?

- Nowhere is this theory more important than when considering human behaviour: looking at an individual human as an atom of behaviour is to miss how behaviour is openly interconnected, not just between themselves but with their environment or context. This was also memorably captured in

John Godfrey Saxe's poem of the 'Six blind men of Indostan' grappling to identify an elephant – where each may have an individually justifiable point of view without grasping the whole

- In the same way, for those who seek enlightenment as to the difference between a product and a brand, perhaps one way of looking at a brand is to hypothesize it as an 'emergent property' of the product: more than just the product's attributes, its parts, its function but something that appears as a higher-order effect

- One other thing to note: try and be as precise with language as possible around scientists. Professionally, they distinguish between 'complex', 'complicated' and 'chaotic' in a way that lay folk tend not to

TAGS: science, language, complexity, brands

48. "NOW THESE THINGS NEVER HAPPENED, BUT ALWAYS ARE"

WHO SAID IT AND IN WHAT CONTEXT

This was originally written by the 4th century writer Flavius Sallustius, in *Concerning the Gods and the Universe.*

To be clear, there are a few Sallusts if you're not in the know. The most celebrated one was Gaius Sallustius Crispus, 85 BCE to 34/5 BCE, a Roman historian, stylist and creator of the monograph *The conspiracy of Catiline*, a study of the war against Jugurtha, and *The Histories*, of which little remains.

And then there's the 5th century Sallustius of Emesa, the Cynic philosopher.

Flavius Sallustius was a consul in 363 BCE and friend of the emperor Julian ('The Apostate' 361-3 CE), who composed a practical handbook which sought to present a unitary understanding of Hellenic paganism as well as the nature of the gods and their role in the universe.

Sallustius' epigrammatic saying suggests that myth works in the abstract and general rather than the specific and at any particular time, because myths have a perpetuity of existence. His saying describes the allegorical nature of mythology and suggests that myths contain behind their often fairy tale and fantastical nature hidden truths and higher meanings.

B) WHY THEY SAID IT

Sallustius' observation was also cited by Carl Sagan in the introduction to his 1977 book, *The Dragons of Eden: Speculations on the Evolution of Human Intelligence*, and more recently by Israeli professor Oren Harman, Chair of the Graduate Program in Science, Technology and Society at Bar-Ilan University in his bridge-building book, *Evolutions: 15 Myths That Explain Our World*.

Harman's book is unlike almost any recent science work, combining an overview of a range of scientific topics in an attempt to re-enchant science by bringing myth, metaphor and lyricism to the stories of creation and mankind's genesis, while remaining within a robustly scientific tradition.

The Canadian literary critic and theorist Northrop Frye wrote in a similar vein to Sallustius, in *The Educated Imagination*:

> *"The poet's job is not to tell you what happened, but what happens: not what did take place, but the kind of thing that always does take place. He gives you the typical, recurring, or what Aristotle calls a universal event."*

c) WHEN YOU SHOULD USE IT

- Sallustius' insight demonstrates how myths and stories work because they embody timeless truths about the human condition. As Harman puts it with typical elegance, "myths summon truths beyond our jurisdiction" and are an "expression of existential conundrums, creatures of our lonely searching minds" in that they express deeply-embedded human truths

- This reminds us that sometimes stories and myths are the most coherent ways of understanding human behaviour. Anyone immersed in the world of business and market research knows that there are profound issues when asking people questions about their individual or tribal behaviour. Perhaps we need to ask people not to remember their behaviour or predict it, but frame it as a story or myth in which the truth will be nestled

- Equally, those bent on hunting down insights should always seek to find the universal in the particular – what I call UHTs, Universal Human Truths

- Some of the smartest and most eloquent scientists are those that can cast the complex and complicated nature of science in a story or myth that resonates deeply and broadly

TAGS: storytelling, myth, research, behavioural economics

49. "SUNLIGHT IS SAID TO BE THE BEST OF DISINFECTANTS"

A) WHO SAID IT AND IN WHAT CONTEXT

Louis Dembitz Brandeis (1856-1941) was an American litigator, the first Jewish Supreme Court Justice, an advocate of privacy and developer of the 'Brandeis Brief'.

His famous analogy appeared in 'What Publicity Can Do', Chapter 5 in *Other People's Money and How the Bankers Use It*. He was highlighting issues relating to investment banks and what he considered to be conflicts of interest within what he termed the 'Money Trust' in a bid to change financial services regulations.

> *"Publicity is justly commended as a remedy for social and industrial diseases. Sunlight is said to be the best of disinfectants; electric light the most efficient policeman."*

(Brandeis' aphorism is the origin of the Sunlight Foundation, a non-partisan, non-profit organization in the US dedicated to using open data and journalism to make government and politics more accountable. He is lauded on their website as *'a trailblazing advocate for civil liberties, individual rights and, yes, sunlight'*.)

One of his many other aphorisms was:

"If we would guide by the light of reason, we must let our minds be bold. We must make our choice. We may have democracy, or we may have wealth concentrated in the hands of a few, but we can't have both."

B) WHY THEY SAID IT

But as is so often the case, scratch beneath the notorious quote and rather more humble and unexpected origins emerge.

James (later Viscount) Bryce (1838-1922) was a jurist and later Liberal MP who served at the International Court at The Hague and supported the establishment of the League of Nations. After several visits to the US, Bryce was sent as British ambassador to Washington in 1907 and presented his findings in *The American Commonwealth*, first published in London in three volumes in 1888, which garnered much acclaim.

In *De La Démocratie en Amérique*, (1835) the French diplomat and historian Alexis de Tocqueville had interpreted American society through the lens of democratic political theory, a work considered to be a forerunner of sociology and political science. A half-century later the Scotsman James Bryce examined 'the institutions and the people of America as they are'.

In Book II, Chapter 87, 'Wherein Public Opinion Succeeds', Bryce first explored the metaphor that Brandeis is almost certainly acknowledging:

"Public opinion is a sort of atmosphere, fresh, keen, and full of sunlight, like that of the American cities, and this sunlight kills many of those noxious germs which are hatched where politicians congregate."

In Book II, Chapter 98, 'Laissez-Faire', he also highlighted an essential characteristic of the American identity:

"And from that day to this, individualism, the love of enterprise, and the pride in personal freedom, have been deemed by Americans not only their choicest, but their peculiar and exclusive possessions."

c) WHEN YOU SHOULD USE IT

- This quotation and the image that it embodies has become a much-quoted touchstone for trust, truth and transparency, frequently cited in support of regulation through disclosure obligations. For instance, former President Obama cited it in order to make promises about trust and open government in a speech from the East Room of the White House in Washington, DC on 28 January 2009

- These days it can be deployed to cover topics such as transparency of standards, accounting and what we would now call data privacy and openness directives, the era of surveillance, government corruption, the banking crisis, WikiLeaks, free speech and 'fake news'. In July 2019, the deputy leader of the UK Labour Party, Tom Watson, commented on the anti-Semitism crisis engulfing the party: *"Only sunlight can disinfect Labour of anti-Semitism now."*

- Oh, and for the non-scientists, it does seem that ultraviolet radiation in sunlight does work as a natural disinfectant: it is used regularly to disinfect drinking water in countries such as India, Kenya and Peru, where more sophisticated forms of water purification are less accessible

TAGS: truth, communications

50. "OOH LOOK, A PIGEON"

A) WHO SAID IT AND IN WHAT CONTEXT

Quite possibly my favourite piece of advertising of all time is a 2003 poster for *The Economist* magazine:

> *'Can you keep people interested or are they easily ooh look, a pigeon.'*

Founded in 1843 by James Wilson on the principles of free trade, internationalism and minimum market interference, *The Economist*'s original mission statement (and how well does this hold up?) was:

> *"To take part in a severe contest between intelligence which presses forward and an unworthy timid ignorance obstructing our progress."*

The famous 'white out of red' campaign was first developed in the 1980s by the newly-appointed advertising agency Abbott Mead Vickers (AMV). In the fight against high-spending national broadsheets, *The Economist* required a highly impactful, clearly branded campaign to cut through the clutter.

According to a former *Economist* publisher, the agency's creative director and copywriting legend, David Abbott, realized that the distinctive red *Economist* masthead was in exact proportion to a 48-sheet poster, which inspired him to develop the celebrated red and white campaign that has since generated hundreds of individual ads and won a multitude of awards.

The first advert Abbott created in the series was:

"'I never read The Economist.' *(management trainee, aged 42)."*

(This predates *The Hitchhiker's Guide to the Galaxy*, so we can only assume the use of 42 is coincidental. See Number 42).

It was smart, incisive and brilliantly branded. Originally copy only, without a tagline or even body copy, it not only defined *The Economist* – it built AMV into one of the UK's largest and most successful agencies and became a benchmark for the type of intelligent advertising that has rarely been emulated.

Abbott himself explained:

"What is potentially a banal positioning line – 'read this and be successful' – is made acceptable and convincing by wit and charm. Things you can't say literally can often be said laterally."

Other highlights of the campaign include:

> 'To err is human. To er, um, ah is unacceptable.'
> 'Would you like to sit next to you at dinner?'
> 'Economist readers welcome – Sperm Donor Clinic.'
> 'In opinion polls, 100% of Economist readers had one.'
> 'Do not fold.'
> 'Not all mind-expanding substances are illegal.'
> 'B#.'

One of the posters even played on one of *The Economist*'s core style principles:

> "A poster should contain no more than eight words, which is the maximum the average reader can take at a single glance. This, however, is for Economist *readers*."

B) WHY THEY SAID IT

The 'pigeon' poster was written by Mark Fairbanks, who had started his career at Ogilvy & Mather (O&M), in 1990. He went on to become a creative director and was the youngest electee to the O&M board and has won over 160 major national and international creative awards to date.

The perfection of the 'Ooh look ...' execution lies in its transformation of a potentially lifeless strategy or brief (reading *The Economist* will make you smarter and more fascinating) into something pithy, graceful and memorable.

On top of that, it is a turn of phrase which resonates with anyone who has ever experienced meeting-tedium or been stuck in a conversation with someone less interesting than them (which is everyone, obviously).

C) WHEN YOU SHOULD USE IT

- The idea of an attention economy has captured the imaginations (and livelihoods) of many working in the marketing and communications world. Economist Herbert Simon labelled attention "a very perishable commodity". In French philosopher Simone Weil's neat turn of phrase, attention is "the rarest and purest form of generosity"

- So why does so much communications material assault and insult our attention? How many emails, billboards, websites, CVs/bios fail to cut through our generously proffered attention in a desperate race to the bottom of attentiveness?

- Elegance and eloquence are not the reserve of authors, writers or poets. The sharpness, simplicity and wit of a good advertising headline or slogan is testament to the power of the right words to penetrate beneath the defences of attention and move us

TAGS: advertising, communication, simplicity

51. "LET'S CALL IT ... ARTHROPODS"

A) WHO SAID IT AND IN WHAT CONTEXT

It was actually said in a meeting sometime in the 1990s by a group of curators at London's Natural History Museum.

Some backstory.

I was working as an account planner (strategist) at one of the many large advertising agencies I toiled at and which no longer exists (several conclusions are available). One of the accounts I was assigned to was the celebrated Natural History Museum and we were having a meeting about a major new exhibition the museum was planning.

"So," began the curators, who saw themselves squarely as the guardians of the Exhibition, the Defenders of Science against the barbarian hordes of vulgarization.

B) WHY THEY SAID IT

Now for those who need a regular fix of taxonomy, an arthropod is an animal with a body made of joined or jointed segments and a protective covering, like a shell, called an exoskeleton. As they have no internal spine they are, inevitably, inveterate invertebrates.

Many different kinds of animals fall into the category known as arthropods, most of them insects or spiders, but the category also covers crustaceans like shrimp, crabs and lobsters.

About 84% of all known species of animals are members of this phylum. They are represented in every habitat on Earth and play a major role in maintaining ecosystems by pollinating, recycling nutrients and scavenging.

So, back to the 1990s where the cool, hipsterish London agency are being stared down by the corps of curious curators: what do these whippersnappers with their hair highlights, reinforced shoulder pads and carefree attitude to the principle of Linnaean taxonomy know about how to launch a major new exhibition so as to ensure maximum numbers and optimum enjoyment and education?

In curatorial terms it was simple: this was an exhibition of a major phylum, arthropods.

So – obviously – it should be called ... 'Arthropods'. Done deal. Nem con. No further questions.

Except.

As an advertising agency planner it was my role to question client assumptions. And in this case, it wasn't too much of a chore.

So, we proposed that it might not be the smartest idea to call an exhibition 'Arthropods!', if it was aimed at bringing in a diverse public, rather than just the Worshipful Tribe of Taxonomists. Calling it 'Arthropods!' might in all likelihood indicate a show dedicated to joint pain and stiffness, which would rather miss the point.

"So, floppy-haired, dungaree-clad, yuppy classicist, how should it be promulgated?" I was asked pretty much to my face.

"Well," I responded, seemingly thinking on my feet but with positively weeks of prior cogitation "given that most people identify the majority of them as things that fly, creep or crawl, why not call it ... *Creepy Crawlies?*"

After some moments to confront their own confirmation bias, they accepted we might have a point.

Weeks later it was confirmed, and 'Creepy Crawlies' went on to become one of the Natural History Museum's most popular and long-running (crawling?) exhibitions.

c) WHEN YOU SHOULD USE IT

- This is another instance of the power of framing (see also Numbers 10, 56 and 65). How the way things – concepts, brands, choices – are expressed can radically affect our perceptions and thereby alter our choices and decision-making. Framing is how things are put (positioned). Framing is really a perceptual process – it is almost never about *what* is said, but more about *how* it is said

- Originally framing was part of Daniel Kahneman and Amos Tversky's 'Prospect Theory'. There are many examples from academic literature and the world of marketing which have embraced it warmly

TAGS: behavioural economics, framing, marketing, communications

52. "PATHEMATA MATHEMATA"

A) WHO SAID IT AND IN WHAT CONTEXT

Literally translated from the Greek as 'sufferings are learnings'. The first word has its roots in words such as empathy, sympathy, apathy, pathology, psychopath and pathetic. All have the fundamental meaning of experience, suffering or emotion. And pathos itself – in the sense of emotion – was considered by Aristotle to be one of the three main elements of persuasion (and beyond), alongside logos and ethos.

One of the most prominent and recent citations was in *Skin in the Game: Hidden Asymmetries in Daily Life*, the 2018 book by former trader and now essayist, researcher and bodybuilder, Nassim Nicholas Taleb. This book is the most recent from the 'Incerto' series of books that propelled him to fame, notably *Fooled by Randomness* and *The Black Swan*.

It sees him at his relentlessly pugnacious and heretical best. Oozing his usual iconoclasm, and more than usual trenchant sideswipes at his intellectual enemies (notably Steven Pinker), he argues that if you have no skin in the game, you shouldn't be in the game. In other words, you should only take advice from people if they have a vested stake or interest in the outcome. The asymmetry in the subtitle refers to the imbalance of risk and reward.

The origin of the Greek proverb seems obscure and occurs in one version in Herodotus' *Histories* (1.207.1), where the words are spoken by 6th century BCE Lydian king, Croesus:

> *"Our sufferings, by their bitterness, became our teachers."*

B) WHY THEY SAID IT
As Taleb states:

> *"When we make bad decisions, our bodies tell us about it, and we learn. The Greeks called this pathemata mathemata, or 'guide your learning through pain.' Those without skin in the game don't feel the pain of their mistakes and thus fail to learn and improve with time."*

There are more contemporary equivalents.

Everyone's favourite/most hated mantra – 'No pain, no gain' – was popularized by Jane Fonda in the 1980s when she became synonymous with the new fad of aerobics. But its origin lies deeper and more unexpectedly in the past.

In *Ethics of the Fathers* (Pirkei Avot) 5: 21, 2nd century Rabbi Ben Hei Hei proclaimed: "According to the pain is the gain" (or 'according to the effort is the reward'). The Rabbi is clearly thinking of religious and spiritual struggles rather than the challenges of the weights room.

In 1834, Benjamin Franklin writes "there are no gains without pains ...' in that year's edition of his annual *Poor Richard's Almanac*.

You can maybe even trace a path to German philosopher, Friedrich Nietzsche's aphorism on resilience: "What doesn't kill you makes you stronger", which later turned up rather unexpectedly in the pop charts as a 2011 song by American singer and winner of inaugural American Idol, Kelly Clarkson.

Or you could try pathemata mathemata's Latin equivalent – *quae nocent docent* – what harms us teaches us, from the *Adagia* of Dutch humanist philosopher Erasmus (1466-1536).

It was also the title of an early poem by Samuel Taylor Coleridge.

C) WHEN YOU SHOULD USE IT

- Pathemata mathemata does have a certain currency on the internet. You can see it being cited when observing a young rabbit trying to eat a stinging nettle; T-shirts are of course available to purchase, as well as beach towels. It also crops up in relation to 'Squidbot', a deep-learning hub for manufacturers, where engineers build and train industrial agents in minutes (me neither)

- There will be no better approach to teaching agents than through pathemata mathemata, we are informed: it is better that agents learn through all information including error and bad information

- Yet, the original Greek has an assonance and elegance which is hard to emulate. It brings with it a veneer of sophistication and classical wisdom

TAGS: Greek, behaviour

53. "MAXIMUM MEANING, MINIMUM MEANS"

WHO SAID IT AND IN WHAT CONTEXT

Abram Games (1914-1996) was a British designer and the subject of an exhibition in 2019 at London's National Army Museum in Chelsea entitled 'The Art of Persuasion', bringing 100 of his posters together for the first time.

If that appears to be a strange location, it is because Games was a wartime designer. The style of his visual communication was used by the British army and beyond to recruit, educate and influence soldiers and civilians alike. Not only can we see a vision of a nation at war and its vision for a post-war future, but more communications professionals and lay-people alike, we can only admire his technique.

B) WHY THEY SAID IT

Games was the creator, designer and copywriter of each poster. Some of his posters proved controversial and, to his dismay, two of his most powerful posters were banned by Churchill and pulped. Promoted to Captain, in 1942 he was appointed 'Official War Poster Artist' and was to be the only person in army history to be given the title.

Games was enormously versatile and also designed stamps and magazine covers, as well as working in mainstream advertising, though he always felt most comfortable promoting causes rather than brands.

In 1953 Games won a competition to design the first animated promotional sequence for the British Broadcasting Corporation (BBC). He made a working model from piano wire, brass and flashing lights, which was filmed and set to harp music. The public fondly nicknamed it the 'Cock-eyed Wonder', 'Bat Wings', 'the Roving Eye' and 'the Thing'.

For this reason, he can legitimately be considered to be one of the 20th century's most seminal designers. His art was a blend of Bauhaus, constructivism and surrealism, but very much his own.

But he is mentioned here for his ability to not just work with design, but with words. His motto was *'Maximum Meaning, Minimum Means'* and for this alone he deserves enormous credit. What is the art of persuasion, the heart of influence and the goal of all communication if not that pithy summary?

c) WHEN YOU SHOULD USE IT

- Games's emphasis on meaning is at the heart of good communication. Not facts, truths, messages – let alone benefits or propositions – but real human, socially constructed and emotionally-mediated meaning

- His was indeed an art, but in this era of big data let's not forget the art that is required to transmute base facts into the gold of meaning

- And art knows that beauty, elegance and simplicity are all inextricably linked, hence 'minimum means'

- The memorable alliteration alone is worth its weight in communication gold

54. "MUST-URBATION"

A) WHO SAID IT AND IN WHAT CONTEXT

Our first reference to 'personal stress relief' (see also number 68) comes from Albert Ellis. Ellis (1913-2007) was ranked the second most influential psychotherapist in history (ahead of Freud). In a 1982 survey of US and Canadian psychologists, *Psychology Today* noted "no individual—not even Freud himself—has had a greater impact on modern psychotherapy."

Ellis is best known as the founder of the rational therapy movement, now known as Rational Emotive Behaviour Therapy (REBT). Around the same time as psychologist Aaron Beck identified three areas that led to psychological distress – I'm no good, the world is bleak, and my future is hopeless – Ellis broke off from traditional Freudian therapy by abandoning extensive introspection into the past of the patient.

Instead he concentrated on the irrational thoughts and behaviours that lead to psychological suffering and the miseries caused by unrealistic expectations.

Part philosophy – he was heavily influenced by Stoics such as Epictetus and Marcus Aurelius – and part problem-solving strategy, REBT is described by online resource Psycom, as *'a pioneering form of cognitive behaviour therapy developed in 1955 ... an action-oriented approach to managing cognitive, emotional and behavioural disturbances.'*

Ellis wrote over 75 books; many of them, bestsellers like *Sex Without Guilt* and *How to Control Your Anxiety Before It Controls You*, became early forerunners for pop psychology.

At the heart of REBT and its later versions such as Cognitive Behaviour Therapy is the need to examine and challenge unhelpful thinking which creates unhealthy emotions and self-defeating/self-sabotaging behaviours. In true Stoic fashion, it is not the actions that affect us but our response to them.

Late in his life in an interview for *New York Magazine* in 2004, Ellis proudly asserted:

"I was the first psychologist ever to say 'fuck' and 'shit' at the American Psychological Association conference."

B) WHY THEY SAID IT

Ellis believed our unjustifiable dependence on three crippling 'musts' created 'must-urbation', and these three were:

a. I must do well and succeed, otherwise people will think me worthless
b. Everyone must act the way I want them to act and must treat me well
c. The world must be easy, and I must always get what I want

Famously abrasive and polemical, Ellis argued that the concept of self-esteem had caused the greatest emotional suffering in the 20th century because it depended to a large extent on factors outside our control (again, classic Stoicism). So, among other actions, we need to dispel as many illusions as we can, acknowledge our (and others') fallibility and our inability to control the universe, fate or destiny (delete as appropriate).

c) WHEN YOU SHOULD USE IT

- An article on the Albert Ellis institute website by Shonda Lackey is cheekily entitled 'Musturbation: Stop Rubbing Yourself the Wrong Way.'

- Ellis demonstrated the power of a snappy bit of wordplay to capture a large amount of information and insights in a compressed, catchy way. It's not entirely unfair to say that the majority of his REBT philosophy can be unravelled within seconds of explaining 'musturbation'

- Storytelling devotees will also observe that he also exploits the 'rule of 3', whereby repetitions in threes and lists of threes seem to be incredibly prevalent and powerful. Think of three blind mice, three wise men, three musketeers and sayings like *veni, vidi,vici* or the French motto *Liberté, Égalité, Fraternité*

55. "SHIBBOLETH"

WHO SAID IT AND IN WHAT CONTEXT

'Shibboleth' is a term that goes back to the Bible and specifically the 'Book of Judges', Chapter 12.

As Frankie Goes to Hollywood once put it, two tribes go to war, in this case the Ephraimites and Gileadites. (These days Gilead is best known as the name of a bio-tech company, or the theocracy at the heart of Margaret Atwood's and TV series, *The Handmaid's Tale*).

The Gileadites are victorious and to ensure none of the opposition get away, devise a cunning plan whereby fleeing Ephraimites are stopped at a bridge and asked to pronounce the word 'Shibboleth'. Since there was no 'sh' sound in their dialect (which must have made parenting a bind), the Ephraimites could only say 'sibboleth' and thus 42,000 of them became victims to this early form of phoneme-testing.

(Younger readers may find it more helpful to watch the Bridge of Death scene in Monty Python *and the* Holy Grail, *or even* Tarantino's Inglourious Basterds,

199

where the British soldier, played by Michael Fassbender, gives the game away by using the wrong fingers when ordering drinks to signal '3', betraying his Britishness.)

From there the term 'Shibboleth' came to refer to a custom, phrase or use of language that acts as a litmus test of belonging to a particular social group or class. By definition, it is used as much to exclude as to include.

B) WHY THEY SAID IT

Most cultures and countries have their identifying linguistic shibboleths. One favourite is a basis for much hilarity between Australians and New Zealanders. The former are convinced that the popular culinary dish 'fish and chips' is pronounced more like 'fush and chups' by their local rivals. For football/ soccer fans one notorious shibboleth is often understanding the offside rule.

In 2007-2008, Colombian conceptual artist Doris Salcedo created a work called Shibboleth at the Tate Modern, London. The piece consisted of a 548-foot-long fissure that bisected the floor of the Tate's lobby space. Her work sought to explore racism, boundaries and exclusion.

It proved particularly popular with Irish tourists who came for the crack.

C) WHEN YOU SHOULD USE IT

- A shibboleth is a smart way of acknowledging the importance of codes, jargon, jokes, totems and even brands

- As we saw before with the 'most Jewish joke ever' (Number 9), as humans we are immensely influenced by the tribal norms which we live by

56. "10% ARE DEAD AFTER 5 YEARS"

A) WHO SAID IT AND IN WHAT CONTEXT

We have talked before about the power of framing in creating perceptual bias in decision-making (see for example 'How's your wife ...', Number 10).

In one notable academic experiment, subjects were asked, "Would you agree to undergo a medical operation if your doctor told you: *'Of those who have this procedure, 10% are dead after five years?'*

"Would it have made a difference if the question had been phrased differently: *'Of those who have this procedure, 90% are alive after five years?'*"

B) WHY THEY SAID IT

Donald Redelmeier of the University of Toronto has researched this extensively: see *Journal of the American Medical Association*, July 1973, 'Understanding Patients' Decisions: Cognitive and Emotional Perspectives', written alongside Daniel *Thinking Fast and Slow* Kahneman and Paul Rozin.

The research concludes that more people (including doctors) agree to undertake the risky procedure if the question is positively framed. The prospect of a 90% chance of living is, for most people, preferable to a 10% chance of dying.

C) WHEN YOU SHOULD USE IT

- Though it may rankle with our self-perceived rationality where information is the same no matter how it is expressed, framing is a salutary reminder that perception is affected by form as much as content

- Whether we are 'sharing content', designing a website or talking to our loved ones, we need to appreciate that there are many ways to skin a cat when it comes to presentation of information

TAGS: behavioural economics, framing

57. "?" ... "!"

A) WHO SAID IT AND IN WHAT CONTEXT

Take this example of the shortest correspondence in literary (or possibly any other type of) history.

After the publication in 1862 of *Les Misérables*, (the book, I sometimes have to remind my students, not the film), French poet and novelist Victor Hugo had gone on holiday but was desperate to know how well his latest work was doing.

So, he sent a telegram to his publisher, Hurst and Blackett.

This was as follows:

"?"

Using the same economy of expression, his publisher replied:

"!"

B) WHY THEY SAID IT

These days *Les Misérables* has ensured Hugo's fame, for the play and the film that followed it.

But the anecdote that concerns us is often told as the exemplar of the world's shortest correspondence. It may – as are so many others – be apocryphal and there are other instances of similarly brief succinct correspondence before that, often asking "?" and "0" (as in nothing).

But there is something satisfying about the "?" ... "!" response.

C) WHEN YOU SHOULD USE IT

- In these days of TMI ('too much information' – see Number 30), the Hugo anecdote should remind us that brevity is indeed the soul of wit, but also a fulfilling and effective way of compressing large amounts of information into something the brain finds rewarding

- So, think how you can reward your audience's brains by something terse and surprising rather than filling it with the usual litany of factoids

TAGS: simplicity, myth, storytelling

58. "WE ARE STATUS-TICIANS"

WHO SAID IT AND IN WHAT CONTEXT

Back to our friend Geoffrey Miller (see Number 21), author of *The Mating Mind*, *Spent* and with Tucker Max *Mate*, and Associate Professor of Psychology at the University of New Mexico, doyen of evolutionary psychology and researcher in sexual selection and polyamory. He is often remembered as the guy who in 2007 published research on lap dancers – along with Joshua Tybur and Brent Jordan – and an article in *Evolution and Human Behaviour*, concluding that they make more money (in tips) when they are ovulating.

But he is cited here for the following devilishly good coinage. (Not jealous at all. Honest.)

In the first chapter of *Spent* ('Darwin goes to the mall'), he argues:

"We are not just intuitive linguists; we are also intuitive **status- ticians***. In each case, evolution has crafted our innate ability to acquire culturally modulated communication skills."*

B) WHY THEY SAID IT

As one of the highest profile evolutionary psychologists and one of the few academics who pursues peacekeeping between academics and practitioners in the consumer/marketing world, he is mercifully tolerant and even supportive of marketing and consumer culture.

His thesis in *Spent* has become very influential in the business world but should be more so: that as consumers our purchases are largely driven by the desire to display personality traits that have been shaped by our evolutionary history. His theory of evolved preferences and sexual signalling suggests the marketing and advertising world have a too naïve view of purchasing, thinking it is fuelled by wealth and status. Instead, he argues we want to display more subtle traits such as kindness, intelligence, creativity and personality.

Taking the evolutionary psychology perspective, he examines the reasons that underlay purchasing decisions, going beyond immediate and self-declared needs to find a biologically-based explanation. The fact that he does so with such playfulness should not be underestimated.

c) WHEN YOU SHOULD USE IT

- In Miller's words, we must always recognize the power of the two Darwinian 'fitness cues' to which we are biologically subject: we spend money on products that display social and sexual fitness

- It never ceases to amaze me how few people in the marketing/branding/communications/website businesses can go beyond the rational, self-proclaimed reasons 'consumers' give for decision-making, rather than the unconscious instincts which so often lie beneath, unspoken and unacknowledged

TAGS: behavioural economics, myth, storytelling, neologism

"THE HUMAN IMAGINATION AND ITS BOUNDLESS ABILITY TO PROJECT MEANINGFUL PATTERNS"

A) WHO SAID IT AND IN WHAT CONTEXT

Writer and journalist Erik Davis called his work, *Tech-Gnosis: Myth, Magic and Mysticism in the Age of Information*, 'a dream-book of the technological unconscious'.

He promised to explore *"a secret history of the mystical impulses that continue to spark and sustain the Western world's obsession with technology, and especially with its technologies of communication."* For Davis, technology was a trickster, mischievous, riddling and thoroughly cross-wired.

But, he is looking at how even at the start of the internet era, our brain was constantly seeking out meaning; an even more daunting task given the scale of what we are swimming in in the modern era.

(Incidentally, Davis followed TechGnosis *with a monograph on Led Zeppelin IV (the album).)*

B) WHY THEY SAID IT

Davis's writing is rich, alluring and occasionally tending to hippy-60s-techno-babble. Witness this description of advertising:

> *"They exploit the rich ambiguities of words, images, identities, commodities and social practices in order to craft protean perspectives, to rupture business as usual and to stir up new ways of seeing and being in a world striated with invisible grids of techno-cultural engineering."*

C) WHEN YOU SHOULD USE IT

- It is Davis's delightful summary of our pattern-seeking instinct that makes him a worthy inclusion. How often are we unaware of the 'random static' of the universe?

- As Michael Shermer, founder of the US Skeptics Society, defines it, we have a tendency to patternicity – an instinct to see patterns in the meaningless to make sense of what seems to be a chaotic and often random universe

- And Bruce Hood, as we saw in Number 28, reveals that our intuitions indicate to us that:
  - › There are no random events or patterns in the world
  - › Things are always caused by intention

> Complexity cannot happen spontaneously but must be a product of someone's plan to design things for a purpose
> And all things are essentially different because of some invisible property inside them

- Anyone who has seen the breathtaking Northern Lights will have felt the temptation to want to make this the creation of a deity rather than the random effect of charged particles from the sun striking atoms in Earth's atmosphere.

TAGS: myth, storytelling, simplicity

60. "THE ENCHANTED LOOM"

Steven Rose in *The Making of Memory* refers to a metaphor from Virginia Woolf's *Orlando* to memory as a seamstress who runs her needle in and out, up and down, hither and thither.

This also puts us in mind of the expressive beauty of Charles Sherrington's description of the brain as an 'enchanted loom'. Sherrington was an English neurophysiologist and a Nobel laureate, for his work on reflexes, as well as responsible for coining the word 'synapse'.

In his Gifford lectures in 1937-1938 and later in *Man on His Nature* he said:

> "The great topmost sheet of the mass, that where hardly a light had twinkled or moved, becomes now a sparkling field of rhythmic flashing points with trains of traveling sparks hurrying hither and thither. The brain is waking and with it the mind is returning. It is as if the Milky Way entered upon some cosmic dance. Swiftly the head mass becomes

212

an enchanted loom where millions of flashing shuttles weave a dissolving pattern, always a meaningful pattern though never an abiding one; a shifting harmony of sub-patterns."

B) WHY THEY SAID IT

At the time Sherrington's analogy was the jacquard loom, considered to be the most complex mechanical device of the early 19th century. Some have argued Sherrington took the mind-as-loom image from a passage in Charles Dickens's *Little Dorrit*.

These days, of course, more age-appropriate metaphors would be available.

C) WHEN YOU SHOULD USE IT

• Apart from anything else, the beauty and elegance of the language is breathtaking

• Admittedly, this was the age when writing skills were more highly valued. Sherrington was also a published poet

• But it reminds us that beauty is not the opposite of logic, even when wielded by scientists, but a form of elevation

• So, always seek language which is memorable, emotional and meaningful

TAGS: storytelling, simplicity

61. "IF"

As we have seen elsewhere with Spartan mothers (Number 27), Spartan bluntness was legendary. We have also examined what might be the shortest correspondence in history, so this incitation may qualify as the briefest (and most pointed) riposte. Laconic even.

B) WHY THEY SAID IT

Around 346 BCE, King Philip of Macedon – father of Alexander (the Great) – was marching into Greece to subjugate the city-states and form an alliance against Persia. He turned his attention to Sparta, sending the following message:

> *"If I win this war, you will be slaves forever."*

In another version, he warned: *"You are advised to submit without further delay, for if I bring my army into your land, I will destroy your farms, slay your people, and raze your city."*

According to both versions, the Spartans' reply was one word:

"If."

A second story (less universally verifiable) indicates that Philip asked the Spartans menacingly whether he should approach them as friend or foe. The reply was, "Neither."

Philip, for either strategic or literary reasons, steered clear of Sparta.

c) WHEN YOU SHOULD USE IT

- Once again, we see the benefits of being terse and concise. Sometimes the tone of a response, especially in the world of geopolitics, can be as important as the content

- As we have seen, the Spartans were famed for their lack of embellishment, and these verbal diplomatic engagements would both fit the Spartans' sense of ethnic pride, as well as signalling this to their allies and enemies

TAGS: Greece, myth, storytelling, simplicity

62. "SMALL, FAR AWAY ..."

A) WHO SAID IT AND IN WHAT CONTEXT

Fans of the cult sitcom, *Father Ted* (1995-1998), written by Arthur Mathews and Graham Linehan, may recognize that moment.

In a caravan, during a downpour, Father Ted is explaining to his gormless sidekick, Dougal, about the concept of depth and perspective (technically known as 'depth perception').

Ted points to some toy plastic cows in front of him and explains.

> *'Okay, one last time. These are small ... but the ones out there are far away. Small ... far away.'*

Dougal is demonstrating his misunderstanding of perspective. He thinks that the toy cows are as big as the real cows outside because they are right in front of him.

B) WHY THEY SAID IT

As well as being one of the most recited scenes (and there are indeed many) from *Father Ted* – it is known to fans as 'small, far away' – it was also the name of the 2011 documentary about the series as part of the 15th anniversary of the show.

The documentary followed *Father Ted* creators Graham Linehan and Arthur Mathews as they returned to Craggy Island on a road trip across Ireland, taking them back to some of the key filming locations from the series.

But apart from being funny, the 'small, far away' works because of the scientific truths it embodies. It's become a meme for perspective illusions: a picture of a meeting held between Vladimir Putin and the President of Azerbaijan, Ilham Aliyev, and President of Armenia, Serzh Sargsyan, in Sochi was gleefully seized on for its odd perspective by fans of *Father Ted* and beyond.

C) WHEN YOU SHOULD USE IT

- It has become not just a meme but a useful cultural tag. Scientists and academics feel no hesitation in using it: witness one paper: *'Small or far away? Size and distance perception in the praying mantis.'* by Vivek Nityananda, Geoffrey Bissianna, Ghaith Tarawneh and Jenny Read

- But it is also a way and gateway to demonstrating the illusion known as the Ames Room. The distorted room illusion is named after the American ophthalmologist Adelbert Ames, Jr, who first constructed this type of room in 1946. He based his design on an original by Hermann von Helmholtz in the late 19th century: within an Ames Room people or objects can appear to grow or shrink when moving from one corner to the other

- How often can/should we use a catchphrase or headline as a way of introducing a complex and perhaps rather 'dull' topic?!

TAGS: TV series, framing, behavioural economics

63. AWFUL ACRONYMS

A) WHO SAID IT AND IN WHAT CONTEXT

Searching after terrible acronyms is hardly taxing: from the Transport Workers And Tautliner Specialists to Senior Housing Assistance Group, to Servicio Hosteleria Industrial de Terrassa, they are easy targets.

But too often in the corporate world, acronyms become depersonalizing jargon, ways to remove the human, emotional and unpredictable from the process of understanding and measuring consumer behaviour. Especially, some of the more egregious TLAs (three-letter acronyms).

B) WHY THEY SAID IT

Some examples from my experience: one of the telecoms companies I worked with talked of RGUs (revenue generating units).

Investopedia defines this as:

'An individual service subscriber who generates recurring revenue for a company. This is used as a performance measure for management, analysts and investors.'

It only dawned on us later that this was a way of describing ... people. First cousin to RGU is ARPU, a metric denoting average revenue per user.

Or take SLF, a pejorative term for air passengers – 'self-loading freight'. Sometimes also referred to as 'self-loading cargo'.

Some commentators on professional pilots' forums see it as just affectionate or humorous, others criticize it as demeaning and indicative of poor customer service levels and how 'PAX' (passengers or customers) are treated as transactions that are something to be processed.

C) WHEN YOU SHOULD USE IT

- Acronyms are so effective because they compress and synthesize, often in an arresting and sparkling manner

- However, too often they are used to avoid the messiness of human behaviour in a misplaced attempt to iron out the kinks in humanity to generate and measure frictionless metrics

- Beware of acronyms that tend toward the demeaning or patronizing. Your audience: in the Olden Days of advertising it was a formula to have the benefits of household products ads extolled by two women, known in the business as 2CK – let's call it euphemistically 2 Chicks in a Kitchen

64. "MEN ARE CALLED CREATURES OF REASON ..."

"Men are called creatures of reason: more appropriately, they would be creatures of habit."

A) WHO SAID IT AND IN WHAT CONTEXT

In *Darwin's Worms*, the British psychoanalyst and writer Adam Phillips again cites one of his heroes, Charles Darwin. (We saw Phillips above in Number 43.)

Phillips is analysing our dependence on habit and – as ever – its effect on our perspective on life and death.

B) WHY THEY SAID IT

But again, this should remind us that the unvarnished truth about human behaviour is that despite maintaining a collective veneer that reason guides our lives and decisions, the main motor behind most of what we do is, in fact, habit (or to use the behavioural economics inflected term, heuristics).

Heuristics are important because they display our brains' dependence on energy effectiveness. The human brain stays energy-efficient and optimal by ensuring it does not reinvent the wheel and reconsider every decision. Instead, it makes much more biological sense for the brain to 'satisfice' in much decision-making by designing paths and then pursuing those it has already established; hence unconscious and efficient habits are more important than we would wish to admit.

C) WHEN YOU SHOULD USE IT

- Other ways of expressing this truth are (in French and source unknown):
  'Le rationnel est l'alibi du désir' (The rational is the alibi of desire)

- And: *"We are but men and use reason as a last resort,"* as Israeli politician Abba Eban remarked ruefully, during the Arab-Israeli war of 1967

TAGS: behavioural economics

65. "MATHEMATICS IS A JOKE"

A) WHO SAID IT AND IN WHAT CONTEXT

Alex Bellos is quite the polymath: best known as the author of the bestselling popular maths books *Alex's Adventures in Numberland* and *Alex Through the Looking-Glass*. Bellos is also *The Guardian*'s maths and puzzles blogger, a regular science presenter on BBC Radio 4 and a curator-in-residence at London's Science Museum, as well as the designer of two mathematics colouring books.

(Kudos to his publisher for renaming his 2010 book *'Here's Looking at Euclid'* in the US.)

Before that, Bellos was *The Guardian*'s foreign correspondent in South America, where he wrote a book on Brazilian football (*Futebol: the Brazilian way of life*) and was Pelé's ghostwriter.

B) WHY THEY SAID IT

In *Through the Looking-Glass*, Bellos remarks that:

> *"Mathematics is a joke. I'm not being funny. You need to 'get' a joke just like you need to 'get' maths. The mental process is the same ... jokes are stories with a set-up and a punchline. You follow them carefully until the payoff, which makes you smile. A piece of maths is also a story with a set-up and a punchline.*
>
> *"We'd usually call a mathematical story a proof and the punchline a theorem ... whoosh you get it!"*

C) WHEN YOU SHOULD USE IT

- Another insightful analogy. For many, especially those who feel undeservedly innumerate, nothing could be less like a joke than maths. After all, maths is hard, it's demanding and seems to be something that a section of the public struggles with throughout their lives

- But Bellos's point is well made and may make it easier for the maths-averse to face their fears: seeing maths not as a challenge of mental complexity but as a way of uncovering truths and gaining your own 'aha!' moment might be a more compelling way of framing maths

- Maybe more connections between 'getting' maths and getting a joke could help us all see more insightful patterns

TAGS: humour, science, simplicity

66. "WHAT'S GOING ON BETWEEN OUR LEGS, WHAT ENGINEER WOULD DESIGN THAT?"

"What's going on between our legs, what engineer would design an entertainment system in the middle of a sewage system? No engineer would design that at all."

A) WHO SAID IT AND IN WHAT CONTEXT

You can find this marvellous description in various of Neil deGrasse Tyson's online appearances or in *Space Chronicles: Facing the Ultimate Frontier*, the anthology covering his various writings relating to the history and future of NASA and space travel in general.

Tyson is another scientific-superstar. Astrophysicist, head of the Hayden Planetarium in New York, he is the recipient of 20 honorary doctorates and the NASA Distinguished Public Service Medal, the highest award given by NASA to a non-government citizen.

Alongside a comedic co-host, coupled with weekly guests drawn from pop culture, this science based talk show, *Star Talk*, targets an audience who never thought to listen to science on the radio or watch in a talk show format.

The mark of any celebrity scientist, he has made many media appearances: in *Batman vs. Superman*, *The Simpsons*, *Family Guy*, *Bojack Horseman* and, among other scientific alumni (such as Stephen Hawking), in two episodes of *The Big Bang Theory*.

B) WHY THEY SAID IT

Tyson has mounted many tirades on what he calls 'Stupid Design' as part of a sustained and witty attack on 'Intelligent Design' and the belief that the universe was designed for us specifically (and by an intelligent designer).

But he also goes on to argue that humans do not appear to be the product of intelligent design. One example he gives is why don't we have a separate hole for eating, speaking and breathing (to avoid the risk of choking). As have dolphins.

C) WHEN YOU SHOULD USE IT

- The power of a striking analogy never ceases to work its magic. As part of his demolition of Intelligent Design, this story/anecdote/metaphor provides a marvellous and memorable caricature

- Rather than merely a statement that the sexual reproduction organs are located so close to those concerned with excretion, he frames it within an amusing analogy

- Its memetic afterlife suggests how it can sum up an entire worldview in a well-chosen and gripping analogy

TAGS: humour, analogy, science

67. "CAPTAIN WAS SOBER TODAY …"

A) WHO SAID IT AND IN WHAT CONTEXT

Stephen Jay Gould (1941-2002) was an evolutionary biologist, palaeontologist and disseminator supreme, who took particular subjects for his column and wove them into a tale of interest, intelligence and detection. Neurologist Oliver Sacks was another example.

Gould was a protagonist in the *Darwin Wars*, fought out in the pages of many books and especially *The New York Times Book Review*, (Andrew Brown's book, *The Darwin Wars* covers much of the territory with an incisive eye).

As well as taking part in a very public dispute with fellow scientist Stephen Jay Gould, Richard Dawkins – a passionate atheist – once derided the Catholicism of journalist Paul Johnson as "an ignominious, contemptible, retarded basis for holding the deepest beliefs of one's life".

In *Life's Grandeur* (1996), released in the US as *Full House*, Gould assesses the statistical biases which lead us to mislead historical change. Much of the book is about baseball batting averages (something I enjoy about as much as a text reminder from the dentist).

Gould begins by exploring the unconscious and unrecognized biases we have in depicting the history of life. In this he criticizes formally correct but limited information drastically yanked out of context.

He proceeds to tell a maritime story. A ship's captain has a particular animosity toward his first mate; so, after the mate gets unusually drunk, he records in the ship's log: 'first mate drunk today'. The mate begged his captain to remove the entry as it was not a typical episode and might jeopardize his career prospects. The captain maintained the vendetta and refused. So, the next day, when it was the first mate's turn to write in the log, he recorded 'Captain was sober today'.

B) WHY THEY SAID IT

Gould's point is that we have a tendency to ascribe too much importance to the exception, the atypical and the outlier. Our storytelling and pattern-seeking brains are fast to look for consistency, but also to alight on the exception that proves the rule.

Take a famous advert created by David Ogilvy, who we saw in Number 14. The campaign was known as 'the man in the Hathaway shirt' and was based on this insight: he asked the aristocratic model whom he had chosen to wear the shirt to sport an eyepatch. The eyepatch created a cryptic sense of mystery and mystique: something that invited the reader to ponder the nature of the incident that had led the character to wear something so noticeable. Advertising thinkers would point to exactly this type of execution to highlight the difference between input (what is actually in the ad) and output (how people seek to decode it).

c) WHEN YOU SHOULD USE IT

- Think of the outlier in both senses. Firstly, the power of the exception should always be something never to be ignored: be careful in case we are only looking at the average or the mean (as I am wont to say, you won't get much meaning from a mean)

- A similar thought came from American physicist John Archibald Wheeler, who helped develop the theory of nuclear fission and popularized the terms 'black hole' and 'worm hole'; *"In any field find the strangest thing, and then explore it."*

- But also ensure that you are not over-reliant on the exception

TAGS: myth, storytelling, framing, simplicity

68. "MEETINGS ARE AN ADDICTIVE, HIGHLY SELF-INDULGENT ACTIVITY"

"Meetings are an addictive, highly self-indulgent activity that corporations and other large organizations habitually engage in only because they cannot actually masturbate."

A) WHO SAID IT AND IN WHAT CONTEXT

Dave Barry describes himself as a professional humourist, ever since he discovered that professional humour was a lot easier than working.

Barry has written more than 30 books, including the novels *Big Trouble*, *Lunatics*, *Tricky Business* and, most recently, *Insane City*. For many years he wrote a newspaper column that was syndicated in more than 500 newspapers across the US.

Of his many gags, aphorisms and comments, the two on meetings are most relevant here.

"If you had to identify, in one word, the reason why the human race has not achieved, and never will achieve, its full potential, that word would be 'meetings'."

B) WHY THEY SAID IT

But the incitation cited above incorporates a truth that anyone who has ever been subjected to an endlessly tedious litany of meetings can't help but affirm.

Meetings are an embodiment of Parkinson's Law of Triviality, also known as the Bike Shed Effect. Parkinson suggested that one of the central weaknesses of meetings is that people don't speak up about the big, complex, important decisions because they're scared of embarrassing themselves or feel they are not up to the challenge; but they still want to feel (and appear) as if they're making some sort of contribution, so they'll make sure to weigh in on topics which are either trivial or a lowest common denominator that everyone can have a say on.

Guardian columnist ('This column will change your life') and author of several non-self-help books, (*Help!* and *The Antidote*), Oliver Burkeman returns regularly to the vexed topic of meetings. He cites a Bain review in *Harvard Business Review* (29 April 2014), where Michael Mankins gathered data from a large corporate and discovered that people there spent *300,000 hours a year* just supporting the weekly executive committee meeting because of the ripple effect of meetings that supported meetings that supported that meeting.

c) WHEN YOU SHOULD USE IT

- Perhaps not always safe for work, but Barry's caustic comment has the virtue of saying what is too often unsaid. Meetings do account for a disproportionate amount of business hours, and often too little discernible benefit. This is not only profoundly disturbing but depressing at an individual level

- Sometimes the rough and tumble of work life and the need to fit into the culture leads to an attritional culture of gratuitous waste and swaggering self-indulgence

- In our bid to speak in human, to avoid obfuscatory jargon in the workplace and beyond, we must all seek to banish this behaviour which doesn't even bring any real pleasure

TAGS: humour, simplicity

59. "PLEASE DON'T FLUSH NAPPIES, SANITARY TOWELS ... DOWN THIS TOILET"

"Please don't flush nappies, sanitary towels, paper towels, gum, old phones, unpaid bills, junk mail, your ex's sweater, hopes, dreams or goldfish, down this toilet."

A) WHO SAID IT AND IN WHAT CONTEXT

This is to be found on toilet seats on Virgin trains.

Yes, toilet seats.

What makes it worthy of inclusion is its pithiness, poise and personality.

Rather than being a straightforward, polished yet dull exposition of facts (don't throw stuff down the toilet), it is a more chatty, talkative and emotional piece of communication that many a marketing director would hesitate to endorse. Because it's on a toilet seat.

But that it precisely what makes it so successful. It doesn't feel like a typical piece of information-transmission, irritatingly didactic and full of facts;

rather it charms and seduces you with its slightly surreal drift and catalogue.

B) WHY THEY SAID IT

This is on a toilet seat (did I mention that?).

Not an all-singing, all-dancing TV commercial extolling the virtues of the Virgin brand, featuring cabin staff, glamorous destinations and a backing track by Muse. Yet, here we are discussing a piece of commercial communication stuck on the lid of a toilet on a train.

And that probably cost less than the cost of the milk sachets that come around on the trolley to put in your hot beverage.

Ticking all the boxes of successful communications: emotionally resonant, memorable, simple and oozing personality that gets through our brains' fact-filters.

Or take the celebrated in-cinema ads for Orange mobile phone from the early 2000s in the UK. Superficially fulfilling the same purpose as a still saying 'please turn off your phone', instead it became a daft, delightful and distinctive campaign featuring the 'Orange Film Funding Board', led by Mr Dresden (Brennan Brown) and his sidekick, Eliot (Steve Furst), who would be judging film ideas from the likes of Sean Astin, Rob Lowe and Carrie Fisher.

With Astin's pitch, despite his attempts to avoid typecasting and do something completely different by pitching a contemporary romance in New York, the Board try and make it an entry (the fourth in the trilogy) in *The Lord of the Rings* franchise ('Lord of the ringtones: return of the phone call').

Amusing, catchy and saying a lot more about Orange than much of their so-called mainstream advertising, they remind us again that playfulness is a much under-estimated characteristic in behaviour change.

C) WHEN YOU SHOULD USE IT

- The universal truth behind the Virgin toilet seat is that gaining compliance is not always best achieved by finger-pointing. We all know we really shouldn't flush any objects down a toilet

- But we also know that we don't like being told these rather uncomfortable truths about our-selves: instead, the natural reaction is to turn the other cheek, dismiss the instruction with a cursory 'I know, I know'. Yet humour and playfulness dis-arm our negativity and bring us along into a 'oh, go on then' mood which is far more likely to cheekily nudge us into acceptance

- And one other implication. The Virgin toilet seat copy is actually longer than it needs to be. Surely shorter and simpler is always better? But in this case, the cumulative crescendo of surrealist silli-ness is precisely what gives it its strength

TAGS: advertising, storytelling, simplicity

70. "MY OTHER HALF"

WHO SAID IT AND IN WHAT CONTEXT

A common English idiom, 'my other half' (or sometimes 'better half') refers to one's soulmate. It is often to be found in promotional material for dating websites, encouraging us to find our perfect match, and maybe even making us feel empty and incomplete without finding our kindred soul.

In current usage, 'soulmate' usually refers to a romantic partner, with the implication of an exclusive lifelong bond.

But the expression has a charmingly bizarre origin. It has an unexpectedly ancient history and we need to return to Plato and his dialogue, *The Symposium*, to find its origin.

(If you want it explained with a mellifluous Irish lilt, there is a link in the notes to actor Aidan Turner's explanation from the BBC Radio 4 *History of Ideas* series.)

B) WHY THEY SAID IT

In ancient Greece, the symposium was a 'drinking together' after a meal, where men (sic) would talk, philosophize and carouse.

Our story takes place within Plato's *Symposium* (composed c. 385-370 BCE), which is less like Plato's usual dialogues and more of a series of monologues. (Recall that these are fictional.)

It takes place at the home of tragedian Agathon, who is celebrating a victory at a dramatic festival, and the story is narrated by Apollodorus. The evening will be dedicated to speeches made in praise of Eros.

The most memorable and weirdest speech comes from the eminent comic poet Aristophanes, a mythological tale about the sexes and the gods.

According to Greek mythology, humans were originally created with four arms, four legs and a head with two faces. These weird, fused and monstrous humans had three sexes, not the two we have today. Some were male in both halves, some were female in both halves, and others were androgynous, with one male half and another female half.

These spherical creatures planned an assault on Olympus, so, fearing their power, Zeus split them into two separate parts, condemning them to spend their lives in search of their other halves (hence homosexual, lesbian and heterosexual).

Since then, says Aristophanes, we are all running around in search of our 'other half' to become complete once more. And that is the meaning of love.

c) WHEN YOU SHOULD USE IT

- So, whether you feel this is the profoundly moving, beautiful and wistful account of finding your eternal soulmate and offers hope that keeps our spirit alive by healing our eternal wound; or an outlandish interlude of comic relief told by people from a distant past in their cups; or a satire on the Greek obsession with creation myths; or a preposterous and offensive tale that stigmatizes single people by bringing divine fury on them – it remains a powerful and timeless story

- So timeless, you can look at any number of Hollywood movies (or Hallmark cards); but for one example, take Cameron Crowe's 1996 romcom *Jerry Maguire*, where Tom Cruise's smitten hero tells Renee Zellweger "You complete me". (She responds equally memorably with "You had me at hello.") Up there with "show me the money!"

- In Spanish, there is an equivalent expression "mi media naranja" (my half orange)

- Perhaps, we would think more deeply (and obliquely) if we seek to cast our thoughts; debates in the form of symposia and myth might be a more insightful and playful way of exploring deep philosophical issues

TAGS: Greek, myth, storytelling, simplicity

AFTERWORD

I hope this anthology of seditious teapots, flat wives and self-loading freight has encouraged you to seek out incitations and make new discoveries and connections, whether in the commercial, educational or personal spheres.

So, before you finally return to the world of the humdrum, the mundane and the pedestrian, let's sum up a few emerging themes to send you on your way with a spring in your step and a fair chance of being discovery-prone.

1. **Beware of taking things at face-value.** We need to accept that we can't know everything about who we are, how the world works or that everything can be explained through facts. Many stories – such as Hemingway's baby shoes and Ogilvy's 'I'm blind' – turn out to be well-intentioned myths. Our 'boundless ability to project meaningful patterns into the random static of the universe'

occasionally leads us to see meaning in the random noise around us. Equally, we must distinguish between jumbo jets – which are complicated but can be broken down and analyzed – with mayonnaise which cannot. And avoid the Fundamental Attribution Error – assuming that personality not context is all that leads us to make our decisions.

2. **As human beings, we need to accept our non-rational shortcomings.** Chris Rock's gag is on the money: when you meet someone for the first time, you're not meeting them – you're meeting their representative. We are not simply a library of facts, declarations and needs: we are a subtle, fallible and fragile compendium of what lies beneath, of what we are barely aware of and an honest assessment of that status would be to everyone's benefit. Let's cherish and nurture those quirks, foibles and eccentricities and not unnecessarily demonize the socially maladroit or painfully posh, but instead celebrate unconventionality.

3. **Let us respect and celebrate emotion, playfulness and creativity.** Follow the guidance of Jed *Line of Duty* Mercurio and *"disguise exposition with 'emotional overlay', so it's rendered undetectable."* Playing with different ideas, disciplines, moods and emotions will always create a more human response: look at the two words Ogilvy (allegedly) added to the blind man's sign, which made all the (emotional) difference.

4. **We all need to accept the importance of humour as the royal road to wit and insight, especially in our working lives.** Seinfeld's joke should also remind us that often in communication what is missing is as vital as what is present or explicit. Too often we are so concerned about what we say, we underestimate the importance of what is left unsaid. Who needs to read textbooks on the illusion of perspective when 30 seconds of *Father Ted* ('small, far away') can do it? How can one joke about homeopathy summarize an entire analysis?

5. **Try and avoid using or allowing others to weaponize jargon.** It is usually a baneful, joyless experience especially in the corporate world, where technical, scientific or grammatical jargon is designed to baffle and bewilder, in order to create and cement exclusive and protective priesthoods. Let's try to use more human, expressive language in its place and ostracize the jargonauts. 'Insecure praise-starved flattery sluts', anyone?

6. **We should do our best to build bridges and avoid the comfort and complacency of sitting in our own bubble of confirmation bias.** We have seen how scientists like Peter Medawar, Dan Gilbert, Geoffrey Miller, Steven Pinker, Oren Harman and Marcus du Sautoy can reach out across the chasm of ignorance and apathy and make their fields and disciplines accessible, fun and desirable. The philosophy of consilience – fostering links between

arts and science – is something that should start
early in schools and develop from there.

7. **Content is not all: form matters as much, if not
more.** In these days of too-much-information, the
ubiquity of Big Data, our seemingly runaway will-
ingness to hand over our data to those who will
analyse us – all this can lead us into an unthinking
'monstrous worship of facts' in Wilde's words and
to hide beneath the data duvet. Don't be ensnared
by the quantity and seductiveness of information
or lust after a single number, like 42: we need to
break the long-standing link between more information and better decisions. Be it road signs or
how we communicate with people with autism,
we need to rethink information and how we
transmit and receive it.

8. **Most specifically, let us venerate simplicity.** In
Abram Games's marvellous maxim, we should all
seek 'maximum meaning, minimum means'. It
may not be quite as minimalist as Victor Hugo's
telegram or the Spartans' 'If', but Occam's razor
should always be our guide to parsimony – things
should not be multiplied beyond the necessary.

9. **Remember the importance of framing.** The Virgin
toilet seat doesn't point fingers in a didactic, hectoring manner – it laughs with you complicitly.
Framing is a core component of the behavioural
economics jigsaw for demonstrating how the

framing of information can make an enormous difference to how it is received and acted upon. Another way in which we constantly undervalue form over content. Just consider Party Cannon going against the conventions of Death Metal posters, the exhibition that was almost called 'Arthropods' or Albert Ellis's memorable three 'musts' of 'musturbation'.

10. **Finally, we should attend to the pleasures to be had from side effects, the oblique and the incidental.** If you have taken anything from these incitations, I hope it is that the feeling of alighting on something unexpected feels like a small neurochemical hit – the moment of surprise, a small 'aha' or 'eureka' – which is the small, pleasurable hit from finding something new and true.

— END —

ACKNOWLEDGEMENTS

Thanks to Liddites Martin, Sara, Susan, Natasha and Bella for the constant support, nudging and all-round tolerance and thoughtful discussion of Arcade Fire.

For the third time a big shout out (if only to embarrass them) to Josh, Zach and Saskia. Thanks again to all those who have supplied Earl Grey tea and sconage (it's jam first, then cream).

Above all to Egg, for pretty much everything else.

LIST OF INCITATIONS

1. *"There is as much difference between us and ourselves as there is between us and others"*
2. *"The monstrous worship of facts"*
3. *"If you disguise exposition with 'emotional overlay', it's rendered undetectable"*
4. *"When you meet somebody for the first time, you're not meeting them …"*
5. *"TFBUNDY"*
6. *"Normal for Norfolk"*
7. *"The Tractor Boys"*
8. *"Knowing Me, Knowing You, Aha!"*
9. *"The Most Jewish Joke"*
10. *"How's your wife?" "Compared to what?"*
11. *"Why have cotton when you can have silk?"*
12. *"That will be $3." "Really, when?"*
13. *"I'm leaving you." "Who is he?"*
14. *"I'm blind, please help."*
15. *"Change your words. Change your world."*
16. *"Gnothi Seauton"*

47. *"A Jumbo jet is complicated, but mayonnaise is complex"*
48. *"Now these things never happened, but always are"*
49. *"Sunlight is said to be the best of disinfectants"*
50. *"Ooh look, a pigeon"*
51. *"Let's call it ... Arthropods"*
52. *"Pathemata Mathemata"*
53. *"Maximum Meaning, Minimum Means"*
54. *"Must-urbation"*
55. *"Shibboleth"*
56. *"10% are dead after five years"*
57. *"?" ... "!"*
58. *"We are Status-ticians"*
59. *"The human imagination and its boundless ability to project meaningful patterns"*
60. *"The enchanted loom"*
61. *"If"*
62. *"Small, far away ..."*
63. *Awful Acronyms*
64. *"Men are called creatures of reason ..."*
65. *"Mathematics is a joke"*
66. *"What's going on between our legs, what engineer would design that?"*
67. *"Captain was sober today ..."*
68. *"Meetings are an addictive, highly self-indulgent activity"*
69. *"Please don't flush nappies, sanitary towels ... down this toilet"*
70. *"My Other Half"*

SOURCES AND REFERENCES

1. "There is as much difference between us and ourselves as there is between us and others":

   a. "Michel de Montaigne," Wikiquote, accessed February 13, 2020, https://en.wikiquote.org/wiki/Michel_de_Montaigne.

   b. Matthew Sharpe, "Guide to the classics: Michel de Montaigne's Essays," *The Conversation*, November 1, 2016, https://theconversation.com/ guide-to-the-classics-michel-de-montaignes-essays-63508.

   c. Nicholas Lezard, "Magnifying the Magnificent," *The Guardian*, August 25, 2007, https://www.theguardian.com/books/2007/aug/25/featuresreviews. guardianreview25.

   d. "PHILOSOPHY – Montaigne," YouTube video, 6:02, The School of Life, March 20, 2015, https://www.youtube.com/watch?v=WLAtXWaz76o.

   e. "Montaigne on the penis," Bathtub Bulletin, accessed February 13, 2020, http://bathtubbulletin.com/montaigne-on-the-penis/.

   f. "Of Sex, Embarrassment, and the Miseries of Old Age, After Montaigne," accessed February 13, 2020, http://aftermontaigne.org/atwan/of-sex-embarrassment-and-the-miseries-of-old-age-after-on-some-verses-of-virgil/.

   g. Julian Baggini, *The Ego Trick*, (UK: Granta Books, 2011).

2. "The monstrous worship of facts":

   a. Mark Vernon, "The monstrous worship of facts," *The Guardian*, March 2, 2010, https://www.theguardian.com/commentisfree/belief/2010/mar/02/ lies-spin-plato-wilde.

   b. "The Decay of Lying: An Observation by Oscar Wilde (1891)," Books & Boots, accessed February 13, 2020, https://astrofella.wordpress.com/2014/08/03/ the-decay-of-lying-oscar-wilde/.

c. "The Decay of Lying," The Victorian Web, accessed February 13, 2020, http://www.victorianweb.org/authors/wilde/decay.html.

d. "SparkNote on *Hard Times*," SparkNotes, accessed February 13, 2020, https://www.sparknotes.com/lit/hardtimes/quotes/.

3. **"If you disguise exposition with 'emotional overlay', it's rendered undetectable":**

a. John Yorke, *Into the Woods* (UK: Penguin, 2013).

4. **"When you meet somebody for the first time, you're not meeting them …":**

a. Telegraph Film, "Chris Rock's funniest jokes," *The Telegraph*, February 18, 2016, https://www.telegraph.co.uk/film/what-to-watch/chris-rock-oscars-funny-quotes-jokes/.

5. **"TFBUNDY":**

a. "Doctor slang is a dying art," BBC News, last modified August 18, 2003, http://news.bbc.co.uk/1/hi/health/3159813.stm.

b. "Medical slang," Boards.ie, accessed February 13, 2020, http://www.boards.ie/vbulletin/showthread.php?p=54721076.

c. Tim Spanton, "Doctors' secret language is revealed," *The Sun*, March 9, 2011, https://www.thesun.co.uk/archives/news/417415/doctors-secret-language-is-revealed/.

d. "Doctor slang is a dying art," BBC News, last modified August 18, 2003, http://news.bbc.co.uk/1/hi/health/3159813.stm.

e. "Medical slang," Boards.ie, accessed March 4, 2020, https://www.boards.ie/vbulletin/showthread.php?p=54721076.

6. **"Normal for Norfolk":**

a. Laurence Cawley and Jodie Smith, "Normal for Norfolk: Where did the phrase come from?" BBC News, April 24, 2016, https://www.bbc.co.uk/news/uk-england-norfolk-36082307.

b. Constance Knox, "Desmond MacCarthy on Normal for Norfolk: It's amazing that so many people watch it," *Express*, July 16, 2017, https://www.express.co.uk/showbiz/tv-radio/828937/Desmond-MacCarthy-Normal-For-Norfolk-Wiveton-Hall-TV-show-BBC.

c. Telegraph Obituaries, "Chloe MacCarthy, star of Normal for Norfolk – obituary," *The Telegraph*, July 6, 2018, https://www.telegraph.co.uk/obituaries/2018/07/06/chloe-maccarthy-star-normal-norfolk-obituary/.

d. Ben Lawrence, "Normal for Norfolk shows the eccentric charm of Desmond MacCarthy – review," *The Telegraph*, July 17, 2017, https://www.telegraph.co.uk/tv/2017/07/17/normal-norfolk-shows-eccentric-charm-desmond-maccarthy-review/.

e. Jasper Rees, "Normal for Norfolk, BBC Two," The Arts Desk, April 14, 2016, https://theartsdesk.com/tv/normal-norfolk-bbc-two.

f. Amanda Williams, "New BBC sitcom set on Norfolk coast starring Russ Abbot and Stephanie Beacham is being filmed 165 miles away in Kent to save money," *The Daily Mail*, August 13, 2014, https://www.dailymail.co.uk/news/article-2723777/New-BBC-sitcom-set-Norfolk-coast-starring-Russ-Abbot-Stephanie-Beacham-filmed-165-miles-away-Kent-save-money.html.

g. "Normal for Norfolk? Feeling an affinity with a long-lost regional soap," CST online, accessed February 13, 2020, https://cstonline.net/normal-for-norfolk-feeling-an-affinity-with-a-long-lost-regional-soap-by-tim-snelson-2/.

h. "Norfolk Famous People," Norfolk Tourist Information, accessed February 13, 2020, http://www.norfolktouristinformation.com/norfolk-tourist-information/norfolkfamouspeople.php.

i. Guy Kelly, "What the f*** are the Fulfords doing now?" *The Telegraph*, June 6, 2017, https://www.telegraph.co.uk/men/the-filter/f-fulfords-now/.

7. "The Tractor Boys":

a. Elliot Furniss, "Debenham: Tribute to football fan who coined 'Tractor Boy' nickname," *Ipswich Star*, September 8, 2011, https://www.ipswichstar.co.uk/news/debenham-tribute-to-football-fan-who-coined-tractor-boy-nickname-1-1016939.

b. Dominic Fifield, "Last orders under the Twin Towers," *The Guardian*, May 6, 2000, https://www.theguardian.com/football/2000/may/06/newsstory.sport6.

c. Peter Raven, "Former top referee – Carrow Road 'most aggressive atmosphere that I've ever encountered'," *Eastern Daily Press*, September 17, 2015, https://www.edp24.co.uk/sport/norwich-city/former-top-referee-carrow-road-most-aggressive-atmosphere-that-i-ve-ever-encountered-1-4236493.

8. "Knowing Me, Knowing You, Aha!":

a. Stuart Husband, "Alan Partridge: his rise and fall (and rise again), as told by his creators," *The Telegraph*, February 25, 2019, https://www.telegraph.co.uk/culture/film/10208780/Alan-Partridge-the-A-ha-moments.html.

b. "Aha Moment," Schott's Vocab, accessed February 13, 2020, https://schott.blogs.nytimes.com/2009/11/12/aha-moment/.

9. "The Most Jewish Joke":

a. "Jtube: Norm Macdonald Live: Jerry Seinfelds Best Jewish Joke," Aish HaTorah, accessed February 13, 2020, http://www.aish.com/j/jt/Jtube-Norm-Macdonald-Live-Jerry-Seinfelds-Best-Jewish-Joke.html.

b. Jenny Singer, "Only 50% Of Forward Staffers Get This Seinfeld Joke – Do You?" *The Schmooze*, July 31, 2017, https://forward.com/schmooze/378644/only-50-of-forward-staffers-get-this-seinfeld-joke-do-you/.

c. Paul Anthony Jones, *Word Drops: A Sprinkling of Linguistic Curiosities* (Elliott & Thompson, 2015).

10. "How's your wife?" "Compared to what?":

a. Daniel Dennett, *Darwin's Dangerous Idea* (US: Simon & Schuster, 1995).

b. Mervyn Rothstein, "Henny Youngman, King of the One-Liners, Is Dead at 91 After 6 Decades of Laughter," *The New York Times*, February 25, 1998, https://www.nytimes.com/1998/02/25/arts/henny-youngman-king-of-the-one-liners-is-dead-at-91-after-6-decades-of-laughter.html.

c. "Understanding Patients' Decisions: Cognitive and Emotional Perspectives," JAMA Network, accessed February 13, 2020, https://jamanetwork.com/journals/jama/article-abstract/407158.

11. "Why have cotton when you can have silk?":

a. George Gershwin, "Rhapsody in Blue," composed in 1924.

b. Woody Allen, *Manhattan* (US: United Artists, 1979).

c. Sarah Sternberg and Emma Thornton, "Recapturing the spirit of Galaxy: the Choose Silk Campaign,"AMV BBDO Marketing Society Awards, 2014, https://www.marketingsociety.com/sites/default/files/thelibrary/Mars%20Galaxy.pdf.

d. Gillian West, "GALAXY brings Audrey Hepburn back to life for new advertising campaign," *The Drum*, February 22, 2013, https://www.thedrum.com/news/2013/02/22/galaxy-brings-audrey-hepburn-back-life-new-advertising-campaign.

e. "Galaxy chocolate advert (UK) 1987 – why have cotton when you can have silk?" YouTube video, 0:42, RowleyMile, June 17, 2008, https://www.youtube.com/watch?v=ua55IcxithE.

f. "Why have cotton when you can have silk," National Trust, accessed February 13, 2020, https://www.nationaltrust.org.uk/arlington-court-and-the-national-trust-carriage-museum/features/around-the-world-with-the-chichesters-exhibition.

12. "That will be $3." "Really, when?":

a. Daniel Gilbert, *Stumbling on Happiness* (US: Alfred A. Knopf, 2005).

b. Eric Jaffe, "Interview: Daniel Gilbert," *Smithsonian Magazine*, May, 2007, https://www.smithsonianmag.com/science-nature/interview-daniel-gilbert-152390035/.

13. "I'm leaving you." "Who is he?":

a. Steven Pinker, *The Language Instinct* (W. Morrow and Company, 1994).

b. Steven Pinker, *The Better Angels of Our Nature* (Viking Books, 2011); *Enlightenment Now* (Viking Books, 2018).

14. "I'm blind, please help":

a. "I'm blind. Please leave my sign alone," Asbury & Asbury, accessed February 13, 2020, https://asburyandasbury.typepad.com/blog/2011/04/im-blind-please-leave-my-sign-alone.html.

b. "Why the World's Greatest Advertising Man Added Four Words to a Beggar's Sign," The Bully Pulpit, accessed February 13, 2020, https://jrbenjamin.com/2014/04/03/how-the-worlds-greatest-advertising-man-boosted-a-blind-beggars-income/.

c. "The Power of Words," About This and That, accessed February 13, 2020, https://tskraghu.wordpress.com/tag/ogilvy/.

d. "E. M. Forster: The Difference Between Story and Plot," Aerogramme Writers' Studio, accessed February 13, 2020, https://www.aerogrammestudio.com/2013/03/04/e-m-forster-the-difference-between-story-and-plot/.

e. "The power of revision & the pathetic appeal," Raw Words Editing, accessed February 13, 2020, https://rawwordsediting.com/category/revision/.

f. "David Ogilvy's Copywriting Technique That Made a Homeless Man's Cup Runneth Over ..." American Writers & Artists Institute, accessed February 13, 2020, https://www.awai.com/2013/02/david-ogilvys-copywriting-technique/.

g. E. M. Forster, *Aspects of the Novel* (UK: Edward Arnold, 1927).

15. "Change your words. Change your world":

a. "Am I being unreasonable to find this video about a blind man totally offensive," Mumsnet, accessed February 13, 2020, https://www.mumsnet.com/Talk/am_i_being_unreasonable/2407461-to-find-this-video-about-a-blind-man-totally-offensive.

b. "The story of 'the story of a sign'," Jackie Barrie, accessed February 13, 2020, http://jackiebarrie.com/the-story-of-the-story-of-a-sign/.

c. "The Story of Jacques Prevert," YouTube video, 1:50, Staggering Media, May 15, 2017, https://www.youtube.com/watch?v=WU3RHGFkX-c.

d. "John Cleese Advert for the BBC TV Licence," YouTube video, 2:34, theredmax, June 4, 2011, https://www.youtube.com/watch?v=bh9hz9wsHgw.

16. "Gnothi Seauton":

a. "Know thyself: still excellent advice, after all these years," Footnotes to Plato, accessed February 13, 2020, https://platofootnote.wordpress.com/2017/10/30/know-thyself-still-excellent-advice-after-all-these-years/.

b. Tom Holland, "The oracle is always right," *The Telegraph*, December 22, 2013, https://www.telegraph.co.uk/culture/books/3608955/The-oracle-is-always-right.html.

c. James Davidson, "I told you so!" *London Review of Books*, December 2, 2004, https://www.lrb.co.uk/v26/n23/james-davidson/i-told-you-so.

17. POVs ...:

a. Jamie Fahey, "Popular orange vegetables and silly synonyms," *The Guardian*, January 6, 2014, https://www.theguardian.com/media/mind-your-language/2014/jan/06/popular-orange-vegetables-silly-synonyms.

b. Jamie Fahey, "The Pov quiz of the year," *The Guardian*, January 6, 2014, https://www.theguardian.com/media/mind-your-language/quiz/2014/jan/06/pov-quiz-of-the-year.

c. Jamie Fahey, "My synonym hell," *The Guardian*, June 2, 2010, https://www.theguardian.com/media/mind-your-language/2010/jun/02/my-synonym-hell-mind-your-language.

d. "The Press: Elongated Fruit," *Time*, August 10, 1953, http://content.time.com/time/magazine/article/0,9171,818655,00.html.

e. "Elongated yellow fruit and fluffy white stuff," English for Journalists, accessed February 13, 2020, https://englishforjournalists.journalism.cuny.edu/2013/11/25/elongated-yellow-fruit-and-fluffy-white-stuff/.

f. Karen B. Haller and Frances Shuping, "The Elongated Yellow Fruit," *JOGNN*, Vol. 22 No. 6: 480, https://www.jognn.org/article/S0884-2175(15)33073-2/pdf.

g. Bryan A. Garner, *The Oxford Dictionary of American Usage and Style* (Oxford University Press, 2000).

h. "Today in elongated yellow fruit," Headsup: the blog, accessed February 13, 2020, http://headsuptheblog.blogspot.com/2014/12/today-in-elongated-yellow-fruit.html.

18. "Entia non sunt multiplicanda praeter necessitatem":

a. "William of Ockham (Occam, c. 1280 – c. 1349)," Internet Encyclopedia of Philosophy, accessed February 13, 2020, https://www.iep.utm.edu/ockham/#H2.

b. "What is Occam's Razor?" Math.ucr, accessed February 13, 2020, http://math.ucr.edu/home/baez/physics/General/occam.html.

c. "Everything Should Be Made as Simple as Possible, But Not Simpler," Quote Investigator, accessed February 13, 2020, https://quoteinvestigator.com/2011/05/13/einstein-simple/.

d. Stephen Hawking, *A Brief History of Time* (Bantam Books, 1988).

19. "Economical with the truth":

a. Richard Norton-Taylor, "From Spycatcher to prime minister: the Malcolm Turnbull I knew," *The Guardian*, September 14, 2015, https://www.theguardian.com/australia-news/2015/sep/14/malcolm-turnbull-spycatcher-lawyer-prime-minister.

b. Anthony Sharwood, "Two moments of legal genius which tell you more about Malcolm Turnbull than anything he's ever done in politics," News.com.au, September 16, 2015, https://www.news.com.au/finance/work/leaders/two-moments-of-legal-genius-which-tell-you-more-about-malcolm-turnbull-than-anything-hes-ever-done-in-politics/news-story/99b294dda251d4c3b7de3a5240c1b42b.

c. John Lyons, "Raging Turnbull," *The Sunday Morning Herald*, September 4, 2014, https://www.smh.com.au/lifestyle/raging-turnbull-20140904-10c7ye.html.

d. "Malcolm Turnbull, from Spycatcher to prime minister," *Financial Times*, https://www.ft.com/content/7b1d455c-5c6e-11e5-a28b-50226830d644.

e. Peter Wright and Paul Greengrass, *Spycatcher: The Candid Autobiography of a Senior Intelligence Officer* (US: Viking, 1987).

20. The Stanford Prison Experiment and the FAE:
   a. Philip Zimbardo, *The Lucifer Effect* (New York: Random House, 2007).
   b. Kim Zetter, "TED 2008: How Good People Turn Evil, From Stanford to Abu Ghraib," *Wired*, February 28, 2008, https://www.wired.com/2008/02/ted-zimbardo/.

21. "We are insecure, praise-starved flattery sluts":
   a. Geoffrey Miller, *Spent* (New York: Viking, 2009).
   b. M. J. Stephey, "Sex Sells. Here's Why We Buy," *Time*, May 21, 2009, http://content.time.com/time/health/article/0,8599, 1900032,00.html.
   c. Dylan Evans, "Spent by Geoffrey Miller," *The Guardian*, August 8, 2009, https://www.theguardian.com/books/2009/aug/08/spent-geoffrey-miller-book-review.
   d. Kate Douglas, "Review: *Spent*: Sex, evolution, and the secrets of consumerism by Geoffrey Miller," *New Scientist*, June 10, 2009, https://www.newscientist. com/article/mg20227121-900-review-spent-sex-evolution-and-the-secrets-of-consumerism-by-geoffrey-miller/.
   e. "Miller's Spent: Sex, Evolution, and Consumer Behavior," Jason Collins blog, accessed February 13, 2020, https://jasoncollins.blog/2011/06/15/ millers-spent-sex-evolution-and-consumer-behavior/.

22. "A holy terror of chance":
   a. "Conversations about the End of Time," Publishers Weekly, accessed February 13, 2020, https://www.publishersweekly.com/978-0-88064-217-0.
   b. Murray Gell-Mann, *The Quark and The Jaguar* (New York: Freeman, 1994).
   c. Erik Davis, *TechGnosis* (New York: Harmony Books, 1998).
   d. William Calvin, *The Cerebral Code* (The MIT Press, 1996).
   e. S. J. Gould, *Conversations About the End of Time* (Fromm Intl, 1998).

23. "We reweave, rather than retrieve":
   a. Daniel Gilbert, *Stumbling on Happiness* (Knopf, 2005).
   b. Israel Rosenfield, *The Strange, Familiar and Forgotten: An Anatomy of Consciousness* (Knopf, 1992).
   c. Steven Rose, *The Making of Memory* (Bantam Books, 1992).
   d. Charles S. Sherrington, *Man on his Nature* (Cambridge University Press, 1942).
   e. Tor Nørretranders, *The User Illusion* (Viking, 1998).
   f. Stuart Sutherland, *Irrationality* (Constable, 1992).
   g. Anthony Stevens, *Private Myths: Dreams and Dreaming* (Harvard University Press, 1997).

24. "Hypotheses are adventures of the mind":
   a. Peter Medawar, *Art of the Soluble* (Methuen, 1967).

b. V. S. Ramachandran, "Life-changing books: The Art of the Soluble," *New Scientist*, April 16, 2008, https://www.newscientist.com/article/dn13700-life-changing-books-the-art-of-the-soluble/.

c. William Reville, "Some science is the art of the soluble, while some depends," *The Irish Times*, February 8, 2001, https://www.irishtimes.com/news/some-science-is-the-art-of-the-soluble-while-some-depends-1.278650.

d. Richard Dawkins, *The Oxford Book of Modern Science Writing* (Oxford University Press, 2008).

e. Alan Hedges, *Testing to Destruction* (IPA, 1974/1997).

25. Eats, Shoots and Leaves – the Oxford Comma:

a. Lynne Truss, *Eats, Shoots and Leaves* (Profile Books, 2003).

b. Callie Leuck, "The Comma That Launched a Thousand Ships," Tin House, January 15, 2014, https://tinhouse.com/the-comma-that-launched-a-thousand-ships-clean/.

c. Warren Clements, "Underestimate the Oxford comma at your peril," *The Globe and Mail*, July 15, 2011, https://www.theglobeandmail.com/arts/underestimate-the-oxford-comma-at-your-peril/article625870/.

d. Louis Menand, "Bad Comma," *The New Yorker*, June 21, 2004, https://www.newyorker.com/magazine/2004/06/28/bad-comma.

e. "The Oxford Comma: Friend or Foe?" Listen and Learn, accessed February 13, 2020, https://www.nola.com/opinions/index.ssf/2017/03/oxford_comma_overtime.html.

f. "The Oxford Comma: Essential or Inconsequential," Oxford Royale Academy, accessed February 13, 2020, https://www.listenandlearn.org/blog/the-oxford-comma-friend-or-foe/.

g. Duncan J. Watts, "Is Justin Timberlake a Product of Cumulative Advantage?" *The New York Times Magazine*, April 15, 2007, https://www.oxford-royale.co.uk/articles/oxford-comma.html.

h. Roslyn Petelin, "Grammarians rejoice in the $10 million comma," *The Conversation*, March 20, 2017, https://theconversation.com/grammarians-rejoice-in-the-10-million-comma-74824.

i. "Persnickety Editors," Language Hat, accessed February 13, 2020, http://languagehat.com/persnickety-editors/.

j. Arika Okrent, "The Best Shots Fired in the Oxford Comma Wars," Mental Floss, January 22, 2013, http://mentalfloss.com/article/33637/best-shots-fired-oxford-comma-wars.

26. "For sale. Baby shoes":

a. "For Sale, Baby Shoes, Never Worn," Quote Investigator, accessed February 13, 2020, https://quoteinvestigator.com/2013/01/28/baby-shoes/.

b. "One Word Stories from Richard Kostelanetz," Flash Fiction, accessed February 13, 2020, http://flashfiction.net/2019/01/31/one-word-stories-richard-kostelanetz-8-12/.

   c.   Joanna Smith, "Everything You Need To Know About Flash Fiction," Medium, March 21, 2018, https://medium.com/@joannasmith008/everything-you-need-to-know-about-flash-fiction-29e2513b4f4a.

27. "With It or On It ...":

   a.   "300 – Come back with your shield or on it," YouTube video, 1:23, salvomag, January 27, 2012, https://www.youtube.com/watch?v=m-wKe0DNdhI.

   b.   "Sayings of Spartan Women," Penelope, accessed February 13, 2020, http://penelope.uchicago.edu/Thayer/E/Roman/Texts/Plutarch/Moralia/Sayings_of_Spartan_Women*.html.

   c.   William Mclaughlin, "Some of the Best Catchphrases Of The Ancient Spartans," War History Online, March 7, 2017, https://www.warhistoryonline.com/instant-articles/best-spartan-laconic-phrases-boldest-wittiest-lines-ever-recorded.html.

   d.   "Top 10 Witty (and Badass) Quotes from Ancient Sparta," Top Tenz, accessed February 13, 2020, https://www.toptenz.net/top-10-witty-badass-quotes-ancient-sparta.php.

   e.   Sarah B. Pomeroy, *Spartan Women* (Oxford University Press, 2002).

28. "Supernatural Contagion" – it's a kind of magic:

   a.   Bruce Hood, *Supersense* (Constable, 2009).

29. "Aliefs":

   a.   Paul Bloom, *How Pleasure Works* (Bodley Head, 2010).

   b.   Bruce Hood, *Supersense* (Constable, 2009).

   c.   Tamar Gendler, "Alief in Action," Mind and Language, Vol. 23, No. 5 (2008): 552-585; "Alief and Belief," Journal of Philosophy, Vol. 105, No. 10 (2009): 634-663.

   d.   "Cognitive Biases: Alief," YouTube video, 3:59, Wireless Philosophy, September 15, 2015, https://www.khanacademy.org/partner-content/wi-phi/wiphi-critical-thinking/wiphi-cognitive-biases/v/alief.

   e.   Ashley Hamer, "Alief Is When You Act in Opposition to Your True Beliefs," Curiosity, February 17, 2017, https://curiosity.com/topics/alief-is-when-you-act-in-opposition-to-your-true-beliefs-curiosity/.

   f.   Oliver Burkeman, "This column will change your life: From alief to belief," *The Guardian*, June 19, 2010, https://www.theguardian.com/lifeandstyle/2010/jun/19/oliver-burkeman-aliefs-beliefs.

   g.   Matthew Hutson, *The 7 Laws of Magical Thinking* (Oneworld Publications, 2012).

30. "Too Much Information":

   a.   "Chelmsford bus gate signs 'confusing drivers' brains'," BBC News, February 8, 2019, https://www.bbc.co.uk/news/uk-england-essex-47175357.

   b.   Oksana Tunikova, "Are We Consuming Too Much Information?" Medium, June 7, 2018, https://medium.com/@tunikova_k/are-we-consuming-too-much-information-b68f62500089.

c. John B. Horrigan, "Information Overload," Pew Research Center, December 7, 2016, http://www.pewinternet.org/2016/12/07/information-overload/.

d. "Statistics," Online Etymology Dictionary, accessed February 13, 2020, https://www.etymonline.com/word/statistics.

e. "Can you make it to the end?" YouTube video, 1:24, The National Autistic Society, March 31, 2016, https://www.youtube.com/watch?v=Lr4_dOorquQ.

f. "Make it Stop." YouTube video, 1:20, The National Autistic Society, March 28, 2017, https://www.youtube.com/watch?v=xHHwZJX67-M.

g. Dan Cable and Julian Birkinshaw, "Too much information?" London Business School, December 4, 2017, https://www.london.edu/lbsr/too-much-information.

31. "Continuous Partial Attention":

a. "Continuous Partial Attention," Centre for Enhanced Teaching & Learning, accessed February 14, 2020, http://unbtls.ca/teachingtips/pdfs/sew/Continuous_Partial_Attention.pdf.

b. Paul Lewis, "Wilfing on the web, the new British pastime," *The Guardian*, April 10, 2007, https://www.theguardian.com/technology/2007/apr/10/news.newmedia.

c. Sam Leith, "Is this the end for books?" *The Guardian*, August 14, 2011, https://www.theguardian.com/books/2011/aug/14/kindle-books.

d. "Distracted From Distraction By Distraction," First Known When Lost, accessed February 14, 2020, http://firstknownwhenlost.blogspot.com/2010/11/distracted-from-distraction-by.html.

e. "Continuous Partial Attention," Linda Stone, accessed February 14, 2020, https://lindastone.net/qa/continuous-partial-attention.

f. Steven Johnson, *Everything Bad is Good for You* (Penguin, 2006).

g. Nicholas Carr, *The Shallows* (W. W. Norton & Company, 2011).

h. Susan Greenfield, *Mind Change*, (Rider, 2015).

i. Saul Bellow, *Humboldt's Gift* (Viking Press, 1975).

32. "The Data Duvet":

a. Anthony Tasgal first coined the phrase 'data duvet' in: "The importance of storytelling in market research," Voxpopme, accessed February 13, 2020, site. voxpopme.com/en/the-importance-of-storytelling-in-market-research.

33. Vinyl Handicapping Cartoon:

a. "Cartoons From the May 25, 2015, Issue," *The New Yorker*, accessed February 14, 2020, https://www.newyorker.com/cartoons/issue-cartoons/cartoons-from-the-may-25-2015-issue.

b. Marc Hogan, "Have We Reached Peak Vinyl?" Stereogum, July 27, 2015, https://www.stereogum.com/featured/have-we-reached-peak-vinyl/.

c. "Spent: Sex, Evolution and Consumer Behavior," Library Thing, accessed February 14, 2020, https://www.librarything.com/work/8112534.

d. "Shopping for Sex: wasteful consumerism and Darwin's theory of sexual selection," Dangerous Intersection, accessed February 14, 2020, http://dangerousintersection.org/2007/02/05/shopping-for-sex-wasteful-consumerism-and-darwin%E2%80%99s-theory-of-sexual-selection/.

e. Tim Harford, *The Undercover Economist* (Little, Brown and Company, 2005).

f. Amotz and Avishag Zahavi, *The Handicap Principle* (Oxford University Press USA, 1997).

g. Geoffrey Miller, *The Mating Mind* (Random House, 2000).

h. Geoffrey Miller, *Spent* (New York: Viking, 2009).

i. Richard Dawkins, *A Devil's Chaplain* (W & N, 2004).

j. Bill Rosenblatt, "Vinyl Is Bigger Than We Thought. Much Bigger," *Forbes*, September 18, 2018, https://www.forbes.com/sites/billrosenblatt/2018/09/18/vinyl-is-bigger-than-we-thought-much-bigger/#34bc58b21c9c.

k. Jon Porter, "Vinyl and cassette sales saw double digit growth last year," *The Verge*, January 6, 2019, https://www.theverge.com/2019/1/6/18170624/vinyl-cassette-popularity-revival-2018-sales-growth-cd-decline.

34. "Isn't she rather small and flat?":

a. Tor Nørretranders, *The User Illusion* (Viking, 1998).

b. "Necker Cube," The Illusions Index, accessed February 14, 2020, https://www.illusionsindex.org/ir/necker-cube.

c. "The User Illusion: Cutting Consciousness Down to Size," Library Thing, accessed February 14, 2020, http://www.librarything.com/work/60932/reviews/123232826.

d. "Notes on The User Illusion, part Two," The Tapir's Tale, accessed February 14, 2020, http://anders.janmyr.com/2009/08/notes-on-user-illusion-part-two.html.

e. Heinz R. Pagels, *The Dreams of Reason* (Simon & Schuster, 1988).

f. "Cows: Small Or Far Away? | Father Ted," YouTube video, 1:15, Channel 4, September 28, 2010, https://www.youtube.com/watch?v=MMiKyfd6hA0.

35. Physics Envy:

a. Lewis Wolpert, *The Unnatural Nature of Science* (Harvard University Press, 1994).

b. Mary Midgley, *Science as Salvation* (London: Routledge, 1992); *The Ethical Primate* (London: Routledge,1994); *Science and Poetry* (London: Routledge, 2001).

c. Steven Rose, *Lifelines* (Oxford University Press, 1997).

36. "Which comes first – the words or the music?":

a. "Sammy Cahn," Songwriters Hall of Fame, accessed February 14, 2020, https://www.songhall.org/profile/Sammy_Cahn.

b. Mark Steyn, "Obituary: Sammy Cahn," *Independent*, January 18, 1993, https://www.independent.co.uk/news/people/obituary-sammy-cahn-1479324.html.

c. Espie Estrella, "Which Comes First, Melody or Lyrics?" liveaboutdotcom, March 6, 2017, https://www.thoughtco.com/which-comes-first-melody-or-lyrics-2457061.

d. "Sammy Cahn on Songwriting," Oxford Songwriting, accessed February 14, 2020, http://oxfordsongwriting.com/sammy-cahn-on-songwriting/.

e. Clive Barnes, "The Theater: 'Words and Music' by Sammy Cahn," *The New York Times*, April 17, 1974, https://www.nytimes.com/1974/04/17/archives/the-theater-words-and-music-by-sammy-cahn-lyricist-leads-an.html.

f. "Capriccio," Wikipedia, accessed February 14, 2020, https://en.wikipedia.org/wiki/Capriccio_(opera).

37. "The opposite of play isn't work, it's depression":

a. "What is 'The Play Ethic'?" The Play Ethic, accessed February 14, 2020, https://www.theplayethic.com/what-is-the-play-ethic.html.

b. Pat Kane, *The Play Ethic* (Macmillan, 2004).

c. Frank Rose, *The Art of Immersion* (W. W. Norton & Company, 2011).

d. Brian Boyd, *On The Origin of Stories* (Harvard University Press, 2011).

e. Simon Hattenstone, "In the name of the father," *The Guardian*, February 28, 2003, https://www.theguardian.com/culture/2003/feb/28/artsfeatures.danieldaylewis.

38. "Ultracrepidarianism":

a. Mark Forsyth, *Etymologicon* (Icon Books, 2011).

b. Mark Forsyth, *The Horologicon* (Icon Books, 2012).

c. Nick Duerden, "The Etymologicon: The little wonder that left its author lost for words," *Independent*, January 24, 2012, https://www.independent.co.uk/arts-entertainment/books/features/the-etymologicon-the-little-wonder-that-left-its-author-lost-for-words-6293561.html.

d. "Ultracrepidarian," Merriam-Webster, accessed February 14, 2020, https://www.merriam-webster.com/words-at-play/polite-words-for-impolite-people/ultracrepidarian.

e. "Ultracrepidarian," World Wide Words, accessed February 14, 2020, http://www.worldwidewords.org/weirdwords/ww-ult1.htm.

f. "'Ultracrepidarian', coined to denigrate a specific person," Word Histories, accessed February 14, 2020, https://wordhistories.net/2018/02/03/ultracrepidarian-meaning-origin/.

39. Party Cannon:

a. "Party Cannon," The Metal Archives, accessed February 14, 2020, https://www.metal-archives.com/bands/Party_Cannon/3540337014.

b. Robert Pasbani, "Have PARTY CANNON Created The Best Death Metal Band Logo of All Time?" Metal Injection, October 2, 2015, http://www.metalinjection.net/around-the-interwebs/have-party-cannon-created-the-best-death-metal-band-logo-of-all-time.

c. Patrick Smith, "This Death Metal Band Has The Least Death Metal Logo Possible," *Buzzfeed*, October 1, 2015, https://www.buzzfeed.com/patricksmith/party-cannon.

    d. Christopher Hooton, "Party Cannon eschew cliched black metal logo for something a little less brutal," *Independent*, October 1, 2015, https://www.independent.co.uk/arts-entertainment/music/news/party-cannon-eschew-black-metal-logo-for-something-a-lot-less-brutal-a6675516.html.

    e. Graeme McMillan, "While You Were Offline: Metal Band Party Cannon Turns Its Logo Up to 11," *Wired*, October 3, 2015, https://www.wired.com/2015/10/week-on-the-internet-42/.

    f. Hanna Flint, "This band totally trolled a poster for a Death Metal Festival," *Metro*, October 1, 2015, https://metro.co.uk/2015/10/01/this-band-totally-trolled-a-poster-for-a-death-metal-festival-5416731/.

    g. "Logo inspiration from death metal band Party Cannon," Civic Web Media, accessed February 14, 2020, https://www.civicwebmedia.com.au/logo-inspiration-from-death-metal-band-party-cannon/.

40. "There are two kinds of people in the world …":

    a. "There Are Two Classes of People in the World; Those Who Divide People into Two Classes and Those Who Do Not," Quote Investigator, accessed February 14, 2020, https://quoteinvestigator.com/2014/02/07/two-classes/.

    b. Steven Pinker, *How The Mind Works* (New York: W. W. Norton & Company, 1997).

    c. "Robert Benchley," Encyclopaedia Britannica, accessed February 14, 2020, https://www.britannica.com/biography/Robert-Benchley.

    d. "Venice: Streets Full of Water. Advise," Quote Investigator, accessed February 14, 2020, https://quoteinvestigator.com/2011/04/20/streets-flooded/.

    e. Bruce Watson, "The Gentle Wit of Robert Benchley," *American Heritage*, accessed February 14, 2020, https://www.americanheritage.com/node/132754.

41. "Anyone can do any amount of work provided …":

    a. Robert Benchley, "How to Get Things Done: One Week in the Life of a Writing Man," *Chicago Tribune*, February 2, 1930.

    b. John Tierney and Roy Baumeister, *Willpower* (New York: Penguin Press, 2011).

    c. Daniel Engber, "Everything Is Crumbling," *Slate*, March 6, 2016, http://www.slate.com/articles/health_and_science/cover_story/2016/03/ego_depletion_an_influential_theory_in_psychology_may_have_just_been_debunked.html?via=gdpr-consent.

    d. "The End of Ego-Depletion Theory?" *Discover*, accessed February 14, 2020, http://blogs.discovermagazine.com/neuroskeptic/2016/07/31/end-of-ego-depletion/#.XHbFk9j7Su4.

    e. "Replicability Audit of Roy F. Baumeister," Replicability-Index, accessed February 14, 2020, https://replicationindex.com/2018/11/16/replicability-audit-of-roy-f-baumeister/.

    f. "Willpower Summary," Four Minute Books, accessed February 14, 2020, https://fourminutebooks.com/willpower-summary/.

g. Hans Villarica, "The Chocolate-and-Radish Experiment That Birthed the Modern Conception of Willpower," *The Atlantic*, April 9, 2012, https://www.theatlantic.com/health/archive/2012/04/the-chocolate-and-radish-experiment-that-birthed-the-modern-conception-of-willpower/255544/.

h. Richard Nordquist, "Robert Benchley on How to Avoid Writing," ThoughtCo., July 3, 2019, https://www.thoughtco.com/how-to-avoid-writing-robert-benchley-1692827.

i. John Perry, *Don't Buy This Book Now!* (Viking, 2013).

j. Oliver Burkeman, "This column will change your life: structured procrastination," *The Guardian*, September 7, 2012, https://www.theguardian.com/lifeandstyle/2012/sep/07/change-your-life-procrastination-burkeman.

k. Alexandra Petri, "How to stop procrastinating," *The Washington Post*, June 27, 2014, https://www.washingtonpost.com/blogs/compost/wp/2014/06/27/how-to-stop-procrastinating/?utm_term=.04fbb25f6e2d.

l. "Benchley Tonight: 'How to Get Things Done'," Down with Tyranny, accessed February 14, 2020, http://downwithtyranny.blogspot.com/2010/01/benchley-tonight-how-to-get-things-done.html.

m. Evernote, "Don't Put it Off: Procrastination," Medium, July 6, 2017, https://medium.com/taking-note/dont-put-it-off-procrastination-27e59d6a7c8d.

42. "42":

a. Paul Bignell, "42: The Answer to Life, the Universe and Everything," *Independent*, February 6, 2011, https://www.independent.co.uk/life-style/history/42-the-answer-to-life-the-universe-and-everything-2205734.html.

b. "42," The Hitchhiker's Guide to the Galaxy Wiki, https://hitchhikers.fandom.com/wiki/42.

c. Peter Gill, "Douglas Adams and the cult of 42," *The Guardian*, February 3, 2011, https://www.theguardian.com/books/2011/feb/03/douglas-adams-42-hitchhiker.

d. "Why is 42 'the answer to the universe'?" The Naked Scientists, accessed February 14, 2020, https://www.thenakedscientists.com/articles/questions/why-42-answer-universe.

43. "Need is the fall guy of desire":

a. Adam Phillips, *Darwin's Worms* (Faber and Faber, 1999).

b. Adam Phillips, *Side Effects* (Hamish Hamilton, 2006).

c. Joan Acocella, "This Is Your Life," *The New Yorker*, February 18, 2013, https://www.newyorker.com/magazine/2013/02/25/this-is-your-life-2.

d. Susanna Rustin, "Adam Phillips: a life in writing," *The Guardian*, June 1, 2012, https://www.theguardian.com/books/2012/jun/01/adam-phillips-life-in-writing.

e. Kate Kellaway, "You know what I mean ..." *The Guardian*, July 24, 2006, https://www.theguardian.com/theobserver/2006/jul/23/society.

   f.   "Charles Darwin and earthworms," Science Learning Hub, accessed February 14, 2020, https://www.sciencelearn.org.nz/resources/22-charles-darwin-and-earthworms.

   g.   "Darwin's Worms," Earthworm watch, accessed February 14, 2020, https://www.earthwormwatch.org/blogs/darwins-worms.

   h.   Abba Eban, cited in Lyall Watson, *Dark Nature: A Natural History of Evil* (Harper Collins, 1999).

44. "We don't serve tachyons here":

   a.   Kate Ravilious, "Doctor, doctor ..." *The Guardian*, September 8, 2005, https://www.theguardian.com/science/2005/sep/08/1?INTCMP=SRCH.

   b.   "Science Jokes," Sympatico, accessed February 14, 2020, http://www3.sympatico.ca/n.rieck/docs/science_jokes.html.

   c.   Keir Mudie, "The world's geekiest jokes explained after Reddit challenge to find most intellectual gag," *Mirror*, July 13, 2013, https://www.mirror.co.uk/news/weird-news/worlds-geekiest-jokes-explained-after-2051303.

   d.   Toby Manhire, "15 of the funniest intellectual jokes," Noted, July 14, 2013, https://www.noted.co.nz/archive/listener-nz-2013/15-of-the-funniest-intellectual-jokes/.

   e.   "What is known about tachyons, theoretical particles that travel faster than light and move backward in time? Is there scientific reason to think they really exist?" Scientific American, October 21, 1999, https://www.scientificamerican.com/article/what-is-known-about-tachy/.

   f.   Steve Jones, *Almost Like a Whale: The Origin of Species Updated* (Doubleday, 1999).

45. Number 45:

   a.   Ian Hislop, "From satirical coins to subversive salt-shakers: a history of political protest through objects," *NewStatesman*, September 5, 2018, https://www.newstatesman.com/culture/2018/09/satirical-coins-subversive-salt-shakers-history-political-protest-through-objects.

   b.   Anna Souter, "1 Object: Ian Hislop's Search for Dissent at the British Museum," The Upcoming, November 27, 2018, https://www.theupcoming.co.uk/2018/11/27/i-object-ian-hislops-search-for-dissent-at-the-british-museum-exhibition-review/.

   c.   Rosemary Hill, "Ian Hislop's Search for Dissent," *London Review of Books*, October 11, 2018, https://www.lrb.co.uk/v40/n19/rosemary-hill/at-the-british-museum.

   d.   Jane Clinton, "Rebel yell," *Camden New Journal*, September 27, 2018, http://camdennewjournal.com/article/rebel-yell.

   e.   "Ian Hislop on dissent: It's cathartic to say, 'This is rubbish'," Newscabal, accessed February 14, 2020, https://www.newscabal.co.uk/ian-hislop-on-dissent-its-cathartic-to-say-this-is-rubbish/.

   f.   "1 object: Ian Hislop's search for dissent," KCW London, accessed February 14, 2020, http://www.kcwtoday.co.uk/2018/09/i-object-ian-hislops-search-dissent/.

g. "John Wilkes," Wikipedia, accessed February 14, 2020, https://en.wikipedia.org/wiki/John_Wilkes.

h. Jack Lynch, "Wilkes, Liberty, and Number 45," Colonial Williamsbury, accessed February 14, 2020, https://www.history.org/foundation/journal/summer03/wilkes.cfm.

46. "What we call rational grounds for our beliefs are irrational attempts to justify our instincts":

a. Charles Darwin, *On the Origin of Species by Means of Natural Selection* (London: John Murray, 1859).

b. T. H. Huxley, "On the Natural Inequality of Man," Popular Science Monthly Vol. 36 (April, 1890).

c. "Thomas Henry Huxley," BBC History, accessed February 14, 2020, http://www.bbc.co.uk/history/historic_figures/huxley_thomas_henry.shtml.

d. "The Great Debate," Oxford University Museum of Natural History, accessed February 14, 2020, http://www.oum.ox.ac.uk/learning/pdfs/debate.pdf.

e. Tom Mullen, "Sir Richard Owen: The man who invented the dinosaur," BBC News, February 26, 2015, https://www.bbc.co.uk/news/uk-england-lancashire-31623397.

f. "On The Natural Inequality of Men," Clark University Department of Mathematics and Computer Science, accessed February 14, 2020, https://mathcs.clarku.edu/huxley/CE1/NatIneq.html#cite13.

g. Richard Nordquist, "Rational, Rationale, and Rationalize,"ThoughtCo., November 12, 2019, https://www.thoughtco.com/rational-rationale-and-rationalize-1689601.

h. V. S. Ramachandran, *Phantoms in the Brain* (Fourth Estate Ltd, 1999).

47. "A Jumbo jet is complicated, but mayonnaise is complex":

a. Paul Cilliers, *Complexity and Post Modernism* (London: Routledge, 1998).

b. "Paul Cilliers understood the nature of complexities," SciBraai, accessed February 14, 2020, https://scibraai.co.za/paul-cilliers-understood-nature-complexities/.

c. Oliver Human, "Oliver Human on Paul Cilliers," Theory Culture & Society, January 20, 2014, https://www.theoryculturesociety.org/oliver-human-on-paul-cilliers/.

d. Erik Davis, *TechGnosis* (Harmony Books, 1998).

e. Steven Rose, *Lifelines* (Oxford University Press, 1997).

f. Paul Cilliers, *Complexity & Postmodernism* (London: Routledge, 1998).

g. "On the Complexity of Mayonnaise," The Hungry Philosopher, accessed February 14, 2020, https://hungryphil.com/2016/11/29/on-the-complexity-of-mayonnaise/.

h. "Stuart A. Kauffman," Edge, accessed February 18, 2020, https://www.edge.org/conversation/stuart_a_kauffman-chapter-20-order-for-free.

i. Mark Oldridge, "The Rise of the Stupid Network Effect," *International Journal of Market Research* Vol. 45, No. 3 (May, 2003): 1–15.

j. "The poems of John Godfrey Saxe/The Blind Men and the Elephant," Wikisource, accessed February 14, 2020, https://en.wikisource.org/wiki/The_poems_of_John_Godfrey_Saxe/The_Blind_Men_and_the_Elephant.

48. "Now these things never happened, but always are":

a. Oren Harman, *Evolutions: Fifteen Myths that Explain Our World* (Macmillan USA, 2018).

b. David B. Green, "The Polymath Who Wrote the History of Science in Poetry," Haaretz, June 15, 2018, https://www.haaretz.com/israel-news/.premium-the-polymath-who-wrote-the-history-of-science-in-poetry-1.6162957.

c. "Sallust," Encyclopaedia Britannica, accessed February 14, 2020, https://www.britannica.com/biography/Sallust.

d. "'The Gods and the World' by Roman Philosopher Flavius Sallustius," Buscando a las Musas Perdidas, accessed February 14, 2020, http://perdidasmusas.blogspot.com/2016/03/the-gods-and-world-by-roman-philosopher.html.

e. "Sallustius," Wikiquote, accessed February 14, 2020, https://en.wikiquote.org/wiki/Sallustius.

f. Carl Sagan, *The Dragons of Eden* (New York: Random House, 1977).

g. Northrop Frye, *The Educated Imagination* (University of Toronto Press, 1963).

h. Pauliina Remes and Svetla Slaveva-Griffin, *The Routledge Handbook of Neoplatonism* (Routledge, 2014), https://books.google.co.uk/books?id=ERcWBAAAQBAJ&pg=PT153&lpg=PT153&dq=sallustius+neo-platonism&source=bl&ots=F7r5Sm0Mz9&sig=ACfU3U0VwjWfh0mYIUV_owPwQXD1K3DBNw&hl=en&sa=X&ved=2ahUKEwjSr5iYmIfhAhXJRxUIHRewAo84ChDoATAAegQICRAB#v=onepage&q=sallustius%20neo-platonism&f=false.

i. "Customer reviews: Sallustius: Concerning the Gods and the Universe," Amazon, accessed February 19, 2020, https://www.amazon.com/Sallustius-Concerning-Universe-English-Ancient/product-reviews/0890055505.

49. "Sunlight is said to be the best of disinfectants":

a. Louis Brandeis, *Other People's Money and How the Bankers Use It* (New York: Stokes, 1914).

b. "Our Namesake: Louis D. Brandeis," Brandeis University, accessed February 19, 2020, https://www.brandeis.edu/legacyfund/bio.html.

c. "Where Brandeis got 'sunlight is the best disinfectant'," Alasdair S. Roberts, accessed February 19, 2020. https://aroberts.us/2015/03/01/where-brandeis-got-sunlight-is-the-best-disinfectant/.

d. Andrew Berger, "Brandeis And The History Of Transparency," Sunlight Foundation, May 26, 2009, https://sunlightfoundation.com/2009/05/26/brandeis-and-the-history-of-transparency/.

e. James Bryce, *The American Commonwealth* (Liberty Fund, 1888).

f. Alexis de Tocqueville, *De la Démocratie en Amérique* (London: Saunders and Otley, 1835).

g. "Viscount James Bryce, *The American Commonwealth*, vol. 2 [1888]," Online Library of Liberty, accessed February 19, 2020, https://oll.libertyfund.org/titles/bryce-the-american-commonwealth-vol-2.

h. "James Bryce, Viscount Bryce," Encyclopaedia Britannica, accessed February 19, 2020, https://www.britannica.com/biography/James-Bryce-Viscount-Bryce.

i. "Sunlight is the Best Disinfectant," Wikisource, accessed February 19, 2020, https://en.wikisource.org/wiki/Sunlight_is_the_Best_Disinfectant.

j. Ciara McCarthy, "Is Sunlight Actually the Best Disinfectant?" *Slate*, August 9, 2013, https://slate.com/technology/2013/08/sunlight-is-the-best-disinfectant-not-exactly.html.

k. Joshua Tauberer, "Sunlight as a Disinfectant," Open Government Data: The Book, last modified August, 2014, https://opengovdata.io/2014/sunlight-as-disinfectant/.

l. "Other People's Money – Chapter V," Louis D. Brandeis School of Law Library, accessed February 19, 2020, http://louisville.edu/law/library/special-collections/the-louis-d.-brandeis-collection/other-peoples-money-chapter-v.

m. "Labour general secretary criticises 'irresponsible' Tom Watson," *BBC News*, July 12, 2019, https://www.bbc.co.uk/news/uk-politics-48959373.

50. "Ooh look, a pigeon":

a. "Legendary campaigns of The Economist," Lecture, https://www.slideshare.net/advertime/the-economist-creative-advertising-presentation.

b. Nik Studzinski, "Best ads in 50 years: The Economist poster that defined the brand and the agency," *Campaign*, November 29, 2018, https://www.campaignlive.co.uk/article/best-ads-50-years-economist-poster-defined-brand-agency/1519024.

c. Olly Comyn, "Broadening the appeal," *InPublishing*, January 1, 2008, https://www.inpublishing.co.uk/kb/articles/broadening_the_appeal.aspx.

d. "Havas WW London Lures Fairbanks from AMV BBDO," Little Black Book, accessed February 19, 2020, https://lbbonline.com/news/havas-ww-london-lures-fairbanks-from-amv-bbdo/.

e. "The Economist," David Abbott Said, accessed February 19, 2020, http://davidabbottsaid.com/abbott/ab-econ.htm.

f. Jade Garrett, "AMV unrolls Economist poster push," *The Guardian*, October 13, 2000, https://www.theguardian.com/media/2000/oct/13/pressandpublishing.advertising.

51. "Let's call it ... Arthropods":

a. "Creepy Crawlies," Natural History Museum, accessed February 19, 2020, http://www.nhm.ac.uk/visit/galleries-and-museum-map/creepy-crawlies.html.

b. Buz Wilson, "What are arthropods?" Australian Museum, last modified January 21, 2019, https://australianmuseum.net.au/learn/animals/what-are-arthropods/.

52. "Pathemata Mathemata":

a. Nicholas Nassim Taleb, *Fooled By Randomness* (Random House, 2001); *The Black Swan* (Random House, 2007); and *Skin in the Game* (Random House, 2018).

b. "*Histories* (Herodotus)," Wikipedia, accessed February 19, 2020, https://en.wikipedia.org/wiki/Histories_(Herodotus).

c. Benjamin Franklin, *Poor Richard's Almanac* (1834).

d. Erasmus, *Adagia* (1500)

e. David M. Wright, "POTW: What Hurts, Teaches – Reflections on a Coleridge Poem," Circe Institute, October 11, 2013, https://www.circeinstitute.org/blog/potw-what-hurts-teaches-reflections-coleridge-poem.

f. "Pathemata Mathemata because no pain no gain," The Keep Calm-o-matic, accessed February 19, 2020, https://keepcalms.com/p/pathemata-mathemata-because-no-pain-no-gain/.

g. "Erasmus," Lumen Learning, accessed February 19, 2020, https://courses.lumenlearning.com/suny-hccc-worldhistory/chapter/erasmus/.

h. Nassim Nicholas Taleb, "On Interventionists and their Mental Defects," *Medium*, April 21, 2017, https://medium.com/incerto/on-neo-cons-and-their-mental-defects-d12685585b11.

i. "pathēmata mathēmata," YouTube video, 0:27, Nigel Verney, July 19, 2017, https://www.youtube.com/watch?v=-dRcvp5zeHI.

j. "Pathemata Mathemata T-Shirt," Tom Nikkola, accessed March 4, 2020, https://tomnikkola.com/shop/apparel/pathemata-mathemata-t-shirt/.

k. "Pathemata Mathemata Beach Towel," Fine Art America, accessed February 19, 2020, https://fineartamerica.com/featured/pathemata-mathemata-ahmad-zaki-khairul-anuar.html?product=beach-towel.

l. Zoe Williams, "Skin in the Game by Nassim Nicholas Taleb review – how risk should be shared," *The Guardian*, February 22, 2018, https://www.theguardian.com/books/2018/feb/22/skin-in-the-game-nassim-nicholas-taleb-review.

m. "Should risk-takers be required to have 'skin in the game'?" *Financial Times*, https://www.ft.com/content/704ee604-1561-11e8-9e9c-25c814761640.

n. "No pain, no gain," Wikipedia, accessed February 19, 2020, https://en.wikipedia.org/wiki/No_pain,_no_gain.

o. "Ethics of the Fathers: Chapter Five," Chabad, accessed February 19, 2020, https://www.chabad.org/library/article_cdo/aid/2099/jewish/Chapter-Five.htm.

p. Rabbi Wesley Gardenswartz, "Our Struggle *is* Our Reward?" Temple Emanuel, December 8, 2012, https://www.templeemanuel.com/wp-content/uploads/2017/08/20121208_WG_StruggleIsReward.pdf.

53. "Maximum Meaning, Minimum Means":

a. "Abram Games (1914–1996)," Artyfactory, accessed February 19, 2020, http://www.artyfactory.com/graphic_design/graphic_designers/abram_games.htm.

b. Peter Geoghegan, "Maximum Meaning, Minimum Means," September 22, 2009, Culture Northern Ireland, https://www.culturenorthernireland.org/features/visual-arts/maximum-meaning-minimum-means.

c.   "Abram Games: Maximum Meaning, Minimum Means," BBC Art and artists, last modified June 30, 2008, http://www.bbc.co.uk/cumbria/content/articles/2008/06/30/artists_abram_games_feature.shtml.

d.   "The art of persuasion: Wartime posters by Abraham Games," National Army Museum, accessed February 19, 2020, https://www.nam.ac.uk/whats-on/art-persuasion-wartime-posters-abram-games.

e.   "War 1940–1945," A. Games, accessed February 19, 2020, https://www.abramgames.com/war.

f.   Rowan Moore, "Abram Games poster designs – in pictures," *The Guardian*, August 23, 2014, https://www.theguardian.com/artanddesign/2014/aug/23/abram-games-poster-designs-in-pictures.

g.   Rowan Moore, "Abram Games, the poster boy with principles," *The Guardian*, August 23, 2014, https://www.theguardian.com/artanddesign/2014/aug/23/abram-games-poster-graphic-design-principles.

54. "Must-urbation":

a.   Arnold Lieber, MD, "Rational Emotive Behavior Therapy (REBT)," Psycom, last modified November 19, 2018, https://www.psycom.net/rebt/.

b.   Michael Foley, *The Age of Absurdity* (Simon & Schuster, 2011).

c.   Shonda Lackey, Ph.D., "Musturbation: Stop Rubbing Yourself the Wrong Way," The Albert Ellis Institute, September 9, 2013, http://albertellis.org/musturbation-stop-rubbing-wrong-way/.

d.   Matt Dobkin, "Behaviorists Behaving Badly," *New York Magazine*, October 28, 2015, http://nymag.com/nymetro/news/people/features/14947/.

55. "Shibboleth":

a.   Quentin Tarantino, *Inglourious Basterds*, Universal Pictures, 2009.

b.   Terry Gilliam and Terry Jones, *Monty Python and the Holy Grail*, UK: EMI Films, 1975.

c.   Margaret Atwood, *The Handmaid's Tale* (McClelland and Stewart, 1985).

d.   Bruce Miller, *The Handmaid's Tale*, TV series, Hulu, 2017.

56. "10% are dead after five years":

a.   Donald Redelmeier, Daniel Kahneman and Paul Rozin, "Understanding Patients' Decisions: Cognitive and Emotional Perspectives," *Journal of American Medical Association* (July 1993).

57. "?" and "!":

a.   Victor Hugo, *Les Misérables* (A. Lacroix, Verboeckhoven & Cie, 1862).

b.   Victor Hugo, *The Hunchback of Notre Dame* (Gosselin, 1831).

c.   Adrienne Lafrance, "A Surprise Twist in the Mystery of the Lost Telegrams," *The Atlantic*, February 5, 2016, https://www.theatlantic.com/technology/archive/2016/02/telegrams-stop-found-stop-kinda/460161/.

d. "Briefest Correspondence: Question Mark? Exclamation Mark!" Quote Investigator, accessed February 19, 2020, https://quoteinvestigator. com/2014/06/14/exclamation/.

58. "We are Status-ticians":

a. Geoffrey Miller, *The Mating Mind* (Random House, 2000).

b. Geoffrey Miller, *Spent* (New York: Viking, 2009).

c. Kate Douglas, "Review: *Spent*: Sex, evolution, and the secrets of consumerism by Geoffrey Miller," *New Scientist*, June 10, 2009, https://www.newscientist. com/article/mg20227121-900-review-spent-sex-evolution-and-the-secrets- of-consumerism-by-geoffrey-miller/.

59. "The human imagination and its boundless ability to project meaningful patterns":

a. Erik Davis, *TechGnosis* (Harmony Books, 1998).

b. Michael Shermer, *The Believing Brain* (Holt, 2011).

60. "The enchanted loom":

a. Steven Rose, *The Making of Memory* (Bantam Books, 1992).

b. Charles S. Sherrington, *The Gifford Lectures* (1937-8); *Man on His Nature* (Cambridge University Press, 1942).

c. Virginia Woolf, *Orlando* (Hogarth Press, 1928).

61. "If"

a. Philip of Macedon in https://www.warhistoryonline.com/instant-articles/ best-spartan-laconic-phrases-boldest-wittiest-lines-ever-recorded.html

62. "Small, far away ...":

a. Arthur Mathews and Graham Linehan, Father Ted (1995-1998).

b. Vivek Nityananda, Geoffrey Bissianna, Ghaith Tarawneh and Jenny Read, 'Small or far away? Size and distance perception in the praying mantis.' https://royalsocietypublishing.org/doi/full/10.1098/rstb.2015.0262

c. "Small, or far away?" The Royal Institution, accessed February 19, 2020, https://www.rigb.org/families/experimental/small-or-far-away.

d. "Meeting with Ilham Aliyev and Serzh Sargsyan," President of Russia, accessed February 19, 2020, http://en.kremlin.ru/events/president/news/46427.

63. Awful Acronyms:

a. "SLF," Urban Dictionary, accessed February 19, 2020, https://www.urbandictionary.com/define.php?term=SLF.

b. "Rumours & News: self loading freight," Professional Pilots Rumour Network, accessed February 19, 2020, https://www.pprune.org/rumours-news/3056- self-loading-freight.html.

c.   Sam Delaney, "Jets, jeans and Hovis," *The Guardian*, August 24, 2007, https://www.theguardian.com/film/2007/aug/24/1.

64. "Men are called creatures of reason …":

a.   Charles Darwin, *Notebook*, (1839).

b.   Adam Phillips, *Darwin's Worms* (Faber and Faber, 1999).

65. "Mathematics is a joke":

a.   Alex Bellos, *Alex's Adventures in Numberland* (Bloomsbury Publishing, 2010).

b.   Alex Bellos, *Alex Through the Looking-Glass* (Bloomsbury Publishing, 2014).

c.   Alex Bellos, *Futebol: the Brazilian Way of Life* (Bloomsbury Publishing, 2002).

66. "What's going on between our legs, what engineer would design that?":

a.   Neil deGrasse Tyson, *Space Chronicles: Facing the Ultimate Frontier* (W. W. Norton & Co, 2012).

b.   "Intelligent Design is Stupid: Neil deGrasse Tyson," YouTube video, 4:57, Colorado Atheist, September 15, 2009, https://www.youtube.com/watch?v=oEl9kVl6KPc.

c.   Kelly Dickerson, "Neil deGrasse Tyson has a hilarious reason for not believing in intelligent design," *Business Insider*, November 8, 2015, https://www.businessinsider.com/neil-degrasse-tyson-god-religion-2015-11?r=US&IR=T.

67. "Captain was sober today …":

a.   Stephen Jay Gould, *Life's Grandeur* (Jonathan Cape, 1996).

b.   Andrew Brown, *The Darwin Wars* (Simon and Schuster, 2002).

68. "Meetings are an addictive, highly self-indulgent activity":

a.   "Homepage," Dave Barry, accessed February 19, 2020, https://www.davebarry.com/.

b.   Oliver Burkeman, *Help!* (Canongate Books, 2011) and *The Antidote* (Farrar, Straus and Giroux, 2012).

c.   Oliver Burkeman, "Sometimes, meetings are just a waste of time," *The Star*, May 5, 2014, https://www.thestar.com.my/lifestyle/books/news/2014/05/05/sometimes-meetings-are-just-a-waste-of-time/.

d.   Oliver Burkeman, "This column will change your life," *The Guardian*, August 16, 2008, https://www.theguardian.com/lifeandstyle/2008/aug/16/healthandwellbeing2.

e.   Michael Mankins, "This Weekly Meeting Took Up 300,000 Hours a Year," *Harvard Business Review*, April, 2014, https://hbr.org/2014/04/how-a-weekly-meeting-took-up-300000-hours-a-year.

f.   Chris Brahm, Greg Caimi and Michael Mankins, "Your Scarcest Resource," *Harvard Business Review*, May, 2014, https://hbr.org/2014/05/your-scarcest-resource.

69. "Please don't flush nappies, sanitary towels ... down this toilet":

a.   "The funniest sign we have seen in ages | Virgin Trains Notice," We Are The City, accessed March 4, 2020, https://wearethecity.com/the-funniest-sign-we-have-seen-in-ages-virgin-trains-notice/.

b.   Ryan Gilbey, "Orange's cinematic ads that are actually worth watching," *The Guardian*, April 4, 2009, https://www.theguardian.com/film/filmblog/2009/apr/06/orange-film-board-adverts.

70. "My other half":

a.   Plato, *The Symposium* (circa 385-370 BCE).

b.   Cameron Crowe, *Jerry Maguire*, USA: Sony Pictures, 1996.

c.   "The Actual Algebra of Finding Your Soul Mate," Brain Pickings, accessed February 18, 2020, https://www.brainpickings.org/2014/09/02/the-science-of-soul-mates-xkcd/.

d.   "The Myth of the Missing Half," YouTube video, 1:43, BBC Radio 4, July 31, 2015, https://www.youtube.com/watch?v=YDvMRvWjl9Q.

e.   "The Crazy And Charming Theory Of Love In Plato's *Symposium*," All That's Interesting, accessed February 18, 2020, https://allthatsinteresting.com/plato-symposium.

f.   Neel Burton, "Platonic myths: The Myth of Aristophanes," Outre monde, September 25, 2010, https://outre-monde.com/2010/09/25/platonic-myths-the-myth-of-aristophanes/.

g.   "Soul Mate Theory 101: The Origin Story Behind The One," Secure Single, accessed February 18, 2020, https://www.securesingle.com/soulmatetheory101theoriginstorybehindtheone/.

h.   "'My better half'...the interesting way Spanish expresses this concept," interfluency, accessed March 4, 2020, https://interfluency.wordpress.com/2015/02/14/my-better-half-the-interesting-way-spanish-expresses-this-concept/.

i.   Jacey Calle, "Searching For Your Other Half And Why It Is Complete Garbage," The Odyssey Online, February 3, 2015, https://www.theodysseyonline.com/searching-other-half-why-complete-garbage.

j.   Firmin DeBrabander, "What Plato can teach you about finding a soulmate," February 13, 2017, https://theconversation.com/what-plato-can-teach-you-about-finding-a-soulmate-72715.

AN INTRODUCTION TO ANTHONY TASGAL

Anthony Tasgal is a man of many lanyards: he runs his own training company and is a Course Director for the Chartered Institute of Marketing, the Market Research Society, the Institute of Internal Communication, and the Civil Service College. He lectures on the topics of storytelling, behavioural economics and insight in the UK, Europe, the US, China, Hong Kong, Australia and the UAE.

Besides this, Tas is an Associate Lecturer at Bucks New University, Nottingham Trent University and Beijing Normal University. He keynotes regularly at international conferences such as the Insights Association conference in New York and the Australian Market Research Society's annual conference in Sydney. He also appears on TalkRADIO's *Business Breakfast* show to discuss marketing and advertising topics and is a long-term ad agency planner.

As well as *InCitations*, Tas is the author of *The Storytelling Book*, the award-winning guide to using storytelling techniques to improve presentations and communication, and *The Inspiratorium*, a compendium of insight and inspiration.